MAKE A
DIFFERENCE

MAKE A
DIFFERENCE

VOLUME 1 *of the* Eagle Leadership Series – Excellence in Relationships

In the lives of those you love,
live with, and lead

Dr. Larry Little

MAKE A DIFFERENCE
In the lives of those you love, live with, and lead

iUniverse books may be ordered through booksellers or by contacting:

iUniverse
1663 Liberty Drive
Bloomington, IN 47403
www.iuniverse.com
1-800-Authors (1-800-288-4677)

ISBN: 978-1-4759-4549-2 (sc)
ISBN: 978-1-4759-4550-8 (hc)
ISBN: 978-1-4759-4548-5 (e)

Print information available on the last page.

iUniverse rev. date: 06/10/2016

CONTENTS

Acknowledgements

Make a Difference has been a vision that I have carried with me for a lifetime. Writing a book that makes a difference in the lives of people was a simple, yet powerful dream of mine that could not have become a reality had it not been for a host of help and wisdom from many others.

Lauren, my "Monkey/Turtle'" daughter, thank you for the inspiration you give me to love life and give back to others. Landon, my "Lion" son, thank you for your living example of determination and commitment to doing the right thing. Melanie, my intelligent "Camel" wife, thank you for your patience with all of the time that this project has taken. Your gift of detail was invaluable in reviewing and editing the content of this book. Thank you for showing your love through your acts of service. I love you. Mom and Dad, thank you for your continued belief in your son and for a home centered on loving God and loving others.

Deborah Gardner, my retired executive assistant, thank you for the hours spent typing the rough drafts of this project. Your loyalty and friendship throughout the years is greatly appreciated. Have fun in this new season of your life! Coach John Knight, thank you for suggesting the name for the book. You are a valued friend.

Melissa Hambrick Jackson, Chief Operating Officer of Eagle Consulting, thank you for the years of partnering together to grow the EC, and for brainstorming the structure and purpose of this book. You are the best, period. The Eagle Consulting team is an incredible group of men and women who are called to make a difference in the lives of others, thank you for allowing me to serve as your leader. I love and appreciate you.

Finally, the most important acknowledgment goes to God, our Creator. Thank you for sending your Son Jesus who demonstrated the highest dimension of love and who continues to make the ultimate difference in peoples' lives.

INTRODUCTION

An older gentleman was walking down a road when he heard a voice calling out to him, "Hey, you! Hey, old man!"

The old man looked around, and on the ground in front of him was a talking frog. The frog spoke again. "If you kiss me, I'll turn into a beautiful princess and stay with you forever!"

The old man picked up the frog and put it into his sweater pocket, then kept walking down the road.

"Hey, old man!" the frog cried out again from the sweater pocket. "I said if you kiss me, I'll turn into a beautiful princess and stay with you forever!"

The old man just kept walking. The frog, getting exasperated, yelled, "What's wrong with you? Just kiss me already, and then you'll have a beautiful princess!"

The old man stuck his hand into his sweater pocket, pulled out the frog and said, "At my age, I'd rather have a talking frog!"

I hope that I never get to a place in my life where I sacrifice a princess for a frog. In other words, I always want to pursue growth, opportunities, and making a difference in the lives of others. I believe that is the purpose of my life, and it is also the purpose of this book. You see, this book is all about people: I want to teach you how to build better relationships with the people you love, live with, and lead. I want to teach you how to make a difference.

Before we get into the meat of building better relationships, allow me to tell you a little bit about how this project came to life. I believe that I have been given a valuable talent: I have the unique ability to surround myself with people who are the best at what they do. In 1999 I used this gift to assemble the very best of the best in The Enrichment Center, a nonprofit organization that provided counseling and/or coaching. Because of the incredible growth and hard work of our team, we have grown into three different but mission-aligned organizations: Eagle Center for Leadership, Eagle Counseling, and the Enrichment Center. We exist to serve those that our team refers to as mainstream America: real people and organizations with real issues, both personal and professional. Our vision is to "provide excellence in counseling and consulting in order to make a difference in the lives of people," and so far we've done just that. Our counseling team consists of licensed, trained therapists who are passionate about walking with all different kinds of people through their seasons of struggle. Our Eagle Center for Leadership team is comprised of seasoned, qualified coaches who understand how to effectively speak into the lives of leaders and their team members to increase leadership capacity at any type of organization. These teams have grown Eagle Counseling into one of the largest counseling centers in the state of Alabama, and Eagle Center for Leadership into one of the most well reputed coaching and leadership development organizations in the nation.

This book, *Make A Difference*, has been used on both the counseling side with countless individuals looking to understand their own personality and improve their personal relationships, and on the Eagle Center for Leadership side with thousands of organizations and leaders wanting to lead their teams and employees better, starting with defining their own leadership philosophy. We have had so many people find value in the contents of this book that it inspired the EAGLE Leadership Series, a four-part book and seminar series that builds on the contents of this book, Part I: *Make A Difference*, and gives insight into creating accountability in Part II: *Influence Through Accountability*, sustaining growth in Part III: *Growth and Leadership*, and repairing damaged relationships in Part IV: *Engage the Disconnect*.

You can find more information about our leadership development services and the EAGLE Leadership Series at the Eagle Center for Leadership website:

www.eaglecenterforleadership.com

The success that we have experienced in counseling, coaching, and leadership development has led to the realization that there is a strong need for an accurate, easily accessible book on relationships. The tools and insights in this book have made a difference for thousands of people who have experienced counseling and coaching services from the Eagle team.

I sincerely believe that this book will help you to build better relationships in every area of your life. Let's begin to learn how.

CHAPTER ONE

UNDERSTANDING YOUR PERSONALITY

The greatest myth about relationships is that they "just happen." The truth is that all relationships are intentional, and all relationships take work and investment. If you are not intentionally investing in your relationships, they will gradually become unhealthy, and eventually the relationship will end.

Relationships are either growing or dying, and these growths or deaths can be positive or negative, but here's the good news: you get to choose which relationships in which you're going to invest! You get to choose which relationships you want to survive. With the right tools, you can make significant improvements in the relationships that are the most important to you.

In reality, our lives are really all about relationships. We need relationships in every area of our lives. A person who maintains supportive, healthy relationships tends to feel healthier, happier, and more satisfied with his or her life. Also, those in strong relationships are less likely to have mental or physical health problems or participate in activities that are bad for their health. Recent studies have shown that people in healthy relationships tend to have a longer life expectancy than those who are lonely. Conversely, those who are in toxic relationships may shorten their life expectancy. The conclusion? Relationships affect us both psychologically and physically. As a human being, you deserve to be healthy and happy. Your relationships play a significant part in this outcome.

This leads us to the million dollar question: **How can I build better relationships?** It all begins with an understanding of four basic personality profiles. I know that you may be thinking at this point, *Oh great, not another personality test*, but stay with me. As a nationally licensed doctoral psychotherapist, I have researched more personality profiles than you can imagine. There are many good personality assessments out there, but the downside to most of these resources is that they are not conducive for use in our everyday lives. In other words, I may take a complicated test and get lots of data on my personality, but I can't apply that knowledge on a practical basis. Therefore the information, no matter how good it is, is useless to me.

That's why this personality test is different. Knowing your results will not only educate you on the type of person you are and why (a goldmine of information in itself!), but also educate you on how to communicate with other personality types. This is the end goal and the ultimate gift of this book.

Why do we even need to know about personalities? All relationships evolve and center on personalities. Our personalities drive our behaviors and thoughts and therefore define and affect our relationships.

To understand what type of personality you have, you must first understand where your personality originates. Who you are is shaped by three different components: your genetics, your environment, and your behavior.

GENETICS

First let's discuss genetics. We are all born with certain personality tendencies. These behaviors aren't set in stone, but are a sort of guideline for the way we instinctually act.

Any parent can testify to this. Consider my two teenagers, Lauren, nineteen, and Landon, seventeen. From the day Landon was born, there was no doubt that my wife and I were going to have children with very different personalities. Landon has always seen the world in black and white, while Lauren thinks in gray. To her, everything is negotiable. Lauren walks right up to the line and puts one foot over it, thinking surely she can push it just a little. Landon, on the other hand, is a strict rule-follower. He will operate within the structure set up for him. There is no walking up to the line for Landon. After all, rules are made to be followed (well, most of the time. He *is* a teenage boy, but you get the idea).

These are two children raised in the same home with the same parents, and yet they have very different personalities. That can only happen because they have different genetic rules that create very different people. It's true that our personalities don't fully develop until we reach our mid-twenties; however, tendencies or traits can be defined at a very early age. This is just one aspect of the personality makeup.

ENVIRONMENT

Environment is another aspect that plays a significant role in your personality. For example, if you lived in a dysfunctional home for years and were subject to chronic or long-term trauma, your personality tendencies will likely be affected. In other words, if you were raised in a home with constant bickering and fighting, you may develop a coping mechanism of "fight or flight" that allows you to emotionally survive in this environment. A flight response could display itself in you as a fear of conflict. On the other hand, your coping mechanism may be a fight response, or an aggressive personality in the face of conflict.

On the flip side, a home that demonstrates a healthy dose of affirmation and discipline will generally create more positive coping mechanisms in its family members. However, don't take this to mean that a family has to be perfect or your kids will develop personality problems! **Remember, perfection is unattainable**. We're only human, and we all blow it sometimes. A healthy home means a home where members love each other

3

and mess up occasionally, but above all commit to be there for each other in both good times and bad. This type of positive behavior is a learning process for parents and children. Have you heard the phrase, "Happiness is not a destination, it's a journey"? The same is true for healthy homes. It's the day-to-day patience, love, and understanding that create a healthy emotional family, not the unreachable goal of perfection.

BEHAVIOR

The third variable in our personality development is our behavior. Behavior is defined as how we respond to our genetics and our environment. **The good news is that our behavior is our choice**. The bad news is that if we don't control our behavior then our behavior will control us. Many times we allow our emotions to drive our behavior, which sets us up for poor decision making. Bad decision making produces an unhealthy environment for both ourselves and those around us. Bad decisions look like this: when I choose to lose my cool with my spouse, children, friends, coworkers, or employees, I create a hostile environment. Now I am not only responding with unhealthy behavior, but I am also affecting the lives of those around me.

Later in this book we will look at taking personal responsibility for our communication and conflict, but now that you've learned about the three factors that shape our personalities (genetics, environment, and behavior), let's get down to the good stuff and begin with an overview of the four personality types.

The main school of thought from ancient times to the present has grouped personality traits into four main categories. Allow me to make a disclaimer at this point: I realize that there are many valid personality profiles, tests, assessments, etc., on the market today. The Jungian model is the most widely-used psychological personality analysis. It stresses the importance of individuation and focuses on the strengths and weaknesses of individual personality types. Another model that is more common among commercially mainstream profiles is the Myers-Briggs. It provides detailed information concerning personalities as defined by its own model. Another similar model is the Keirsey, which refers to personality types as temperaments. Additionally, in 1971, J. Block created a model that identified five personality types. His model has been researched and revised in recent years and is also considered mainstream. As you can see, there are numerous personality assessments and models. However, in an effort to develop a simple and practical way to understand personality traits that can apply in your everyday life, I developed the ENRICH personality profile assessment. Each personality type is referred to by an animal code name. It may seem a little silly, but using animal names allows us to easily remember the personality tendencies of those we live with, love and lead, instead of using a complicated labeling system.

After you learn which "animal" personality you are, we will discuss your personality assessment in the context of a horizontal and vertical continuum that reveals the DNA of your personality, as well as those of your significant relationships. We will learn how different personalities handle conflict and how to successfully navigate conflict conversations with each one. Finally, I will share with you the essential gifts that are needed for you to make a difference in the lives of others.

While you're taking this personality test, please remember that this tool is not a statistically valid instrument (although after I developed it I tested it on my family and it seemed to work well!). However, The Enrichment Center team has used this tool in the counseling and consulting process on literally thousands of people, and it has proven to be a very good source of self-awareness.

Also, please do not use this tool as a way to label people. We all have our own, unique personalities, and scoring as one animal or another does not mean you will share all of that animal's characteristics or behavior patterns. However, if you have knowledge of common personality traits, you can better understand why we respond and behave the way we do. An understanding of these personality traits will also allow you to better connect and communicate with those around you. As we jump into this overview, be aware that as a human being you are a combination of all these personality types, but generally there are two main personality types from which you operate.

Are you ready to discover your animal and learn how to use this knowledge about your personality to improve your relationships?

1. Go to: www.eaglecenterforleadership.com
2. Click on "Take the Test"

Take your time on this test, as the more thought you put into it the more accurate your answers will be! By the way, the questions do get harder as you go along; it's not your imagination! Keep on choosing the best word that describes you. Thinking carefully about your answer is encouraged, not frowned upon!

Generally, your top two scores will define how you respond in various situations. Did you score in the double-digits on a particular trait? If so, you are what we call a "thoroughbred" personality. That means that you may operate out of that trait in most situations. However, remember that the most important thing is not how you scored, but how this test helps you to gain self-awareness of your personality tendencies.

Are you ready to make sense out of your animal scores? Read below for an overview of the four ENRICH personality animals; keep reading for some in-depth understanding, of each animal and what inspires, motivates, and makes or breaks us:

Much-Loved Monkey. If you are a Monkey then you love to be around groups of people because you are people oriented. You love to laugh and have a good time wherever you find yourself. Monkeys believe that one of the most important things in life is to enjoy the journey! If it's not fun, then the Monkey is not interested. The Monkeys you know generally raise the energy level when they're around. Monkeys bring the party. When they walk through the door, you know "the fun has arrived."

Next is the **Leading Lion**. If Monkeys are people oriented, the Leading Lion is task oriented. Lions are all about getting the job done. If you're a Lion, then you care a lot about the bottom line. You really don't care if others like what you say or not. Lions generally have very strong opinions about a lot of things. They are task oriented. If you give a Lion a task and you get in his way, then you will definitely get run over by his drive to complete the task. Lions paint with a big roller because they want to get the job done—meaning they get to the end as quickly as possible. Lions want to accomplish the BIG task.

So now you have an overview of Monkeys, who are people oriented, and their opposite, Lions, who are all about big tasks. Now we have **Competent Camels.** Camels are task oriented as well, but Camels are focused on small tasks. If the Lions paint with a big roller to get the job done, then Camels paint with the small artist brush to fill in the details. If you are a Camel, then you are a processor. You care much more about how the job gets done than if the job gets done. You're a list maker. Camels love the details of life. When you think of Camels, think of accountants or engineers who are very structured and who find value in the process.

Finally we have the **Tranquil Turtle.** Turtles are laid-back, easy-going individuals, but instead of being people oriented like the Monkey, if you are a Turtle then you are person oriented. You care about one-on-one interpersonal relationships. You're not going to get in a hurry, and you'll do things on your own time. Turtles don't mind being alone and need only a limited number of relationships to feel happy. They don't mind working behind the scenes, but they do mind being singled out or put on the spot in a public setting. Turtles also have a lot of wisdom that can be used to gain great insight into complicated situations.

Now you have a basic awareness of the four personalities (but remember that we are all a combination of these traits). Later, we will look at the ENRICH continuum model that will illustrate our personality quadrant, but for now let's dig a little deeper into each ENRICH animal personality and begin to develop a foundational understanding of the four personality types.

CHAPTER TWO

MUCH-LOVED MONKEY

*"Let us be grateful to people who make us happy, they are
the charming gardeners who make our souls blossom."*
—Marcel Proust

Let's talk about the **Much-Loved Monkey**.

PEOPLE SKILLS

One of the greatest strengths of the Much-Loved Monkey is his
or her people skills. Not only do Monkeys love to have fun, but
they are generally fun to be around as well. Because of their people
orientation, Monkeys have what I call "discernment." This means
that a Monkey can look you in the eye and know when you're
hurting, when you're lonely, or when you're happy. Monkeys are
normally extroverted and have a natural connectivity with others.
They have huge hearts, which translates into authentically caring
about others. When Monkeys sense that something is wrong
with someone, they want to help because of their large capacity
for compassion and empathy.

COMMUNICATION

Monkeys understand how to connect, how to relate, and how to communicate. They are generally verbal and use their people skills to process and problem-solve. In other words, they tend to think out loud and love to brainstorm ideas with others. On a personal level, Monkeys will process their emotions verbally. This means that many times their thought processes should not be taken literally, as they are gray thinkers and may verbalize many options and ideas before landing on an actionable decision.

REJECTION

Monkeys also struggle with feeling rejected, and here's why: Monkeys deeply hear and value words. They strongly internalize what you say to them. For example, let's say Angela is a Monkey. If I said "Angela, sweetie, as your friend I gotta tell you that dress really isn't your color. It really doesn't look good on you. Maybe you shouldn't wear such bright patterns."

This would collapse Angela's world. Angela would respond, "What? You don't like my dress? You don't like what I'm wearing? You must think I'm fashion illiterate. You think I was raised by parents who didn't care about me or how I dressed. You think I'm a horrible person. You think I don't know how to dress or function or . . ." and on and on Angela would spiral into doubt and unhappiness. My comment would ruin her entire day because she would take my rejection of her wardrobe very personally.

To put this into context, if Angela were a Lion and you made that same comment to her, the conversation would likely go like this:

I would say to Angela, "Hey Angela, I'm not sure that dress is your color."

Angela would then say to me, "Oh yeah? I really don't give a rip what you think. I'm not wearing it for you. I don't care that you think it's ugly. I think you're ugly and so is your mother," and then Angela would continue about her day totally unaffected by my comment.

While this example is a large generalization and shouldn't be taken literally, it does illustrate the difference between Monkeys and Lions. I can't emphasize enough that Monkeys deeply connect to words and are easily rejected. We all need to be mindful of what we say to the Monkeys in our lives.

ORGANIZATION

Monkeys are not naturally organized. I'm not saying that if you're a Monkey then you are unorganized; I'm saying that you have to expend energy to become organized. It just doesn't come naturally for you. Organizational skills seem mandatory for Camels, but Monkeys aren't hardwired to be organized, and can generally deal with chaos well. To stay organized, Monkeys have to do one of two things: (1) expend an awful lot of energy to become organized, or (2) surround themselves with people who are naturally organized (like the Camel) and who can help with organization. Once organized, Monkeys can generally keep it going, even though it will not be an enjoyable task for them.

PERSPECTIVE

Before we go any further, there are a couple of myths that we need to address. Myth #1 is that everyone views the world from the same value perspective as you. Myth #2 is that others view you the same way you view yourself.

Let's take a look at Myth #1 as it applies to Monkeys. Monkeys believe that the most important values a person can obtain center around being happy, joyful, verbal, having fun, loving everyone, and making sure that everyone loves them. They have a value system that is people driven and places a lot of importance on enjoying the journey of life. Suppose a Lion is roaring, giving orders, and being concerned with the bottom line, or picture a Camel spinning on the details of a task, being critical, and setting high expectations of others, or if a Turtle is so laid back that he or she isn't motivated to have high energy, or is not interested in a long dialogue. Consequently, the Monkey may not value these individuals or place an importance on maintaining a healthy relationship with them. This devaluing can cause significant damage in a relationship and will facilitate miscommunication and a lack of understanding between both the Monkey and the other animals. But don't worry; I'm going to teach you how to avoid damaging your relationship.

Myth #2 is a common perception within all personalities: surely everyone sees me the same way I see myself, right? Monkeys see themselves as lovable, likeable, and lots of fun, but other personalities have a much different view of our dear Monkeys. Lions may see Monkeys as weak, soft, too nice, too talkative, and needy. Camels may see Monkeys as loud, always late, too silly, distracted, unable to follow through, and not detailed enough. Turtles may see Monkeys as having too much energy, a lack of focus, saying yes without drawing boundaries, and talking needlessly. Meanwhile, the Monkey is wondering why he or she continues to "get on the last nerve" of the other three animals.

It is important to understand and value the diversity of personalities that exist, and it is wise to learn how others may view our own personality traits. This is the first step in the process of developing long-lasting, healthy relationships, as well as mutual understanding and respect. I may not agree with you or your actions, but if I understand your personality makeup, I can better relate to and connect with you on many more levels than are possible if I just write you off. Couples in marriage relationships would do well to gain an understanding of each other's personality tendencies and then accept the truth that you cannot change your spouse's personality. This opens the door for a new and exciting journey for the couple. Now the couple spends less energy on trying to change one another and more energy on speaking each other's language. This translates into acceptance and tolerance for each other. A willingness to connect with your spouse or loved one in a way that he or she can hear will yield incredible benefits.

STRESS

Let's continue with our study of the Much-loved Monkey. How do Monkeys deal with stress? For our conversation, the stressor that we will use for each personality will be that the house is on fire. That's a pretty big item on the stress scale, and believe it or not, each personality is going to react differently to such an extreme emergency. Imagine the following scenario:

The Monkey is at home, and of course he's hanging out with a group of friends. Suddenly he discovers that his house is on fire. The Monkey's natural reaction to this unforeseen obstacle is to say, "Hey guys check this out! A new barbeque pit! This is no problem; it's just a small setback to our party. Everybody keep on having a good time! This is no big deal."

This is an exaggerated example, but it illustrates the Monkey's general response to stress. Their motto is "It's no big deal." Monkeys tend to deemphasize the importance of a negative situation, and use humor as a means to deal with such an occurrence. While this can be helpful at some times, it can also cause frustration for others who recognize the seriousness of the situation. Monkeys should be aware of these tendencies and work to identify the serious nature of stressful situations.

On an emotional level, Monkeys may deny the serious hurt of others if their efforts insure that "everyone is ok and having a good time." Monkeys need to give themselves permission not to emotionally rescue others. The truth is that we cannot have a good time all the time and sometimes the right thing to do is to allow others to experience their emotional pain. Because of the big-hearted nature of the Monkey, this concept is hard to grasp.

Let's go back to the Monkey's use of humor, which can be a strength when used in moderation. When humor is overused, it can become a source of frustration for others. Humor is a wonderful way to defuse tension and raise the comfort level in many situations. However, be careful, Ms. Monkey, and don't use humor when it's inappropriate. Remember, with humor timing is everything.

Consider another example. Anthony, a Monkey, is married to Denise, a Camel. Denise experiences stress or anxiety about a number of things in their lives. Anthony thinks the best way to help Denise is to make jokes or change the subject and try to refocus Denise on something other than her stressor. Unfortunately, that is not what Denise needs. She feels like Anthony is making fun of her stress or that he is minimizing a situation that is very serious to her. This leads to major communication problems. Anthony feels that she is always negative and critical, while Denise begins to not trust Anthony with her emotions. They spiral downward until their marriage sadly ends with both people feeling misunderstood and invalidated. Even sadder is the fact that if they had just taken the time to understand one another's personalities and chosen to invest in making a difference, this marriage could have been saved.

Later, I'll give you powerful and essential gifts for making a difference in the lives of those you love, live with, and lead who are Monkeys, but for now let's move on to understanding the Leading Lion.

CHAPTER THREE

LEADING LIONS

"No one can get inner peace by pouncing on it."
—Harry Emerson Fosdick

BIG TASK PEOPLE

Leading Lions are those people who fly at thirty thousand feet. They see the forest, not the trees. A Lion focuses on the destination, not the journey, and has no problem envisioning where he's headed. Lions focus on their tasks and stay the course until they reach their goal. They are not afraid to take risks, because the end result is squarely in their sights. Being generally extroverted, Lions move fast and furiously and do not like being idle. Lions generally look like leaders because they can see and enjoy the tasks that are required to accomplish the vision set before them. However, keep in mind that while leading may come more naturally to Lions, all personalities can lead. We'll talk more about that later. Lions have strong personalities and are generally capable of making quick decisions. They are prone to "tell it like it is" in order to get the job done. If you are a Lion personality reading this book, you would be much more comfortable if I arranged the content in bullet-point format so that you could read the major points and move on . . . so for all you Lions out there, I will outline your section with bullets:

15

• COMMUNICATION

There is a filter between our brains and our mouths, but many times Lions choose not to use this filter. This results in others being offended or hurt. Lions can be very insensitive to this hurt because words are not important; words are simply tools for completing a job. Lions generally say what they think, and that is not always a good thing. Lions that are wise will learn that while *they* may not be sensitive, others *are* sensitive to words and tone. Once a Lion receives a goal or task, he will work, work, work until he accomplishes the task and reaches his goal. But, if you look at the path the Lion took to accomplish his task, you will see that it may be littered with ruined relationships. The result of this is that while the Lion has achieved his main goal of completing the task, he has caused irreparable damage to others. These damaged relationships will affect his or her ability to accomplish future tasks, as well as cause emotional and personal damage to the victims of the Lion's lack of sensitivity.

• RELATIONSHIPS

Lions may have to remember that people are more important than tasks. After all, if you take people out of the relationship equation, you will truly have nothing left, because relationships are all about people. It takes a minimum of two people to have a relationship. It takes a minimum of two people working together to have a healthy relationship. Healthy relationships means taking the time to understand, love, and lead those for whom you care. In a healthy relationship both investors choose to work towards the following things at any given time: developing an understanding of each other, loving each other unconditionally, and leading each other in specific areas. Yes, Mr. or Ms. Lion, I said you must allow *others* to lead *you* from time to time. If you choose to stay in the leader's mindset all of the time, you will invalidate those around you. We are all gifted in different areas;

therefore it is vital that Lions allow others to use their unique skills or gifts in relationships. This concept applies to personal as well as professional relationships.

Let's use a family relationship for an example: Neil is a Lion and enjoys being in charge at home. His favorite phrase is, "I am the head of this house and while you are in my house you will do as I say." While that makes Neil feel large and in charge, this attitude causes the rest of his family to feel invalidated and frustrated. It also causes his family to lose respect for this man who is husband to one and father to several. On the other hand, what would it look like if Neil invests in his home with the attitude of "We are a family and we all have important roles to fulfill"? In this situation, each person is encouraged to find his or her unique gift and use it. In our home, my wife, Melanie, has a degree in accounting, so she is in charge of our financial accounting and bookkeeping. My daughter, Lauren, who has a love for animals, is in charge of taking care of our dog, cat, and all of the other pets she brings into our home (which has included hermit crabs, rabbits, guinea pigs, etc.). My son Landon loves computers (gaming, the Internet, etc.), so he is in charge of the IT components in our home—keeping the Internet up and running, downloading new software as needed, teaching us how to put our family pictures on the computer, etc. I am in charge of penning the birthday and special occasion poems and cards. I know what you are thinking now: *That sounds really nice, but in the real world there are many responsibilities and chores that must be taken care of in a home that may not be in someone's gift area.* To that I say . . . you are exactly right! Melanie still has to grocery shop and plan meals. Landon still has to take out the garbage and help me with the yard work. Lauren still has to vacuum the floors and clean the bathrooms. I still have to maintain our automobiles. The point is that we all contribute and use our gift sets as well. Don't read this and think, "What a perfect family." We have our struggles just like every other family. However, we also choose to love each other, and we are willing to invest in our family relationship by working to understand and lead each other.

You will never arrive at a perfect relationship. Remember, *perfect* is impossible. It's the journey that is important. To become happier you must simply make a choice to give and invest and work towards healthier relationships.

• WORKAHOLIC

Speaking of work, Lions are also frequently workaholics. They will task all day at work, then come home and start looking for more tasks to accomplish. Here's what it may look like when a Lion who is leading a work team is given a task to accomplish. Let's say this Lion understands our animal personality assessment tool, so she brought a Camel on the team for the details, a Monkey for the people skills, and a Turtle for wisdom. This team works well together and is making great strides and accomplishing a lot. Finally, the Lion-led team accomplishes a very difficult task within their organization. So, what happens next? The Monkey is ready to go have some fun. The Camels are just burned out from all the details they have covered. The Turtles need to have some chill-out time. But instead of celebrating the victory with the team, Lions simply look for another task to accomplish, and then immediately point the team towards another goal. There is no time allowed for celebrating. When you don't celebrate, your team becomes bitter, frustrated, and burned out.

Here's a real-life example. I was working as an executive coach for a very powerful Lion leader. He had assembled an incredibly gifted team who could "rock and roll" when it came to accomplishing big tasks for their organization. Then, after a time, this Lion became frustrated when his team started to underperform. I served as the leadership coach for his team and took them through the ENRICH leadership process, which includes our personality assessment tool. After realizing the DNA personality makeup of his team, the Lion realized that he had not appropriately celebrated his team's victories. Knowing his own strengths and weaknesses, he realized that he just did not have it within himself to celebrate victories. He also realized that celebration was vital to the success of others on his team. So, he did what all great leaders do . . . he surrounded himself with others who had strengths in areas that were his weaknesses. The result was that every few months I would receive a phone call from the Lion leader that went like this: "Larry, we've just accomplished the project. It was a big deal. We need your help in celebrating this victory so I can get on the next task!" The result was a team that became reenergized and continued to accomplish great things while maintaining their Lion's hunger for frequent achievement.

It is important for Lions to understand that while they may not have a need to celebrate; their teams *do* need to celebrate. Remember, it's not about you, it's about people. Celebration is very important. Celebrate the victories.

• PERCEPTION

Let's take a look at the two myths as they apply to the Lion personality:

Myth #1: Everyone shares our own values. Lions value strength and the ability to make decisions quickly. Maintaining confidence, looking at the big picture, asserting dominance, demonstrating power, and being aggressive are among the qualities that Lions value. Here comes a Monkey swinging from tree to tree, saying yes to multiple tasks while trying to please and take care of everyone. Picture the Camel spinning on details, living in the weeds and asking question after question. Finally, along comes the Turtle who needs time to process and ponder the task and is moving at his own pace. What does the Lion have a tendency to do? Most likely, she will roar over those personalities who have a different value system! The result is that relationships are weakened and Monkeys, Camels, and Turtles feel invalidated.

Myth #2: Everyone views us the same way that we view ourselves. Lions view themselves as strong leaders who can get the job done. Monkeys, however, tend to view Lions as having few people skills and little regard for others. Camels may view Lions as running over and through the details while not having a true concern for the quality that they find so important. Turtles may view Lions as rude, arrogant, and not interested in authentic relationships.

A thoroughbred Lion may respond with, "I don't care what others think about me. I know I'm doing fine because my tasks are getting done." Thus Lions fall prey to their common misconception that people are not important. This leads to an important question: How can you make a real difference in someone's life unless you are aware of how that person perceives your behavior? **It is important to realize the significant difference between modifying your behavior just to please others and understanding how your personality affects those around you.** Once you understand their perception of you, the question must be answered, "Do I want to positively impact this person's life?" If the answer is yes, then the process of investing in the relationship begins.

I recently had the opportunity to conduct a leadership conference at the State of Alabama Judicial Building for judges that preside across the state. As we covered the personality awareness portion of the seminar, it was evident that the participants were engaged and interested in increasing their understanding of personalities. I will never forget the comments of one particular judge that came toward the end of our session. He said, "I have spent a lot of time studying and understanding the law and how it is applied. However, I have not stopped to think about how those I lead and live with are affected by my personal value system. I assumed that was a black and white issue and that everyone had the same value system as I. This personality awareness has been eye opening for me and will be a great asset in my personal life as well as in my position on the bench."

Think about the difference this judge will make in the lives of others because of his increased awareness.

• STRESS

Okay, now let's talk about how our Leading Lions handle stress. Remember our stressful scenario that the house is on fire? Upon recognizing that the house is burning, our Lion leaps into action! He calls 911 and is in total control of the situation. When the fire truck arrives, the Lion begins to shout orders to the firefighters: "Get that hose over here! You go around to the back of the house! You get that ladder set up!" Never mind that the Lion has never had one day of training in firefighting. He feels he knows what needs to be done, how it needs to be done, and when it needs to be done, and to a Lion, that always means NOW! Lions respond quickly to crisis situations and have no problem making decisions in the heat of battle. Lions under stress need to remember to allow others to contribute. While Lions certainly have the talent for making decisions in the heat of the moment, their first impulse may not always be the best course of action.

Take a step back, Mr. Lion, and look before you leap. Use the resources around you and empower others to invest or lead in appropriate situations. In relationships, Lions must be constantly aware of their tendency to dominate and intimidate others. In a crisis, aggression is not always the best response.

Here's a real-life example. A friend of mine whom we'll call Michael was totally bewildered. He was on the brink of losing his wife and his family. The main issue was his behavior toward his family. Michael would bark orders to the teenagers then give commands to his wife. His motto was, "In our house we run a tight ship." To my Lion friend this represented order and security for the family. To Michael's wife and children it felt like domination and invalidation. He became more aggressive in times of stress or crisis, so the family began to avoid him whenever they could. When the family was all together, the rest of its members walked a tight rope around Michael. Finally, I had a hard conversation with him that went something like this: "Michael, your perception of what is happening is not correct. Your family feels that they are being dominated by you because of your behavior. If you choose to continue with this way of communicating and continue to ignore your family's emotional needs, you will lose them. You must choose to work toward understanding who your family is and what each one needs from you emotionally. True leadership means true servanthood. In other words, if you are going to save your family, you must *serve* your family, and do what's best for them. The choice is yours." While Michael didn't like or agree with everything I said, he did commit to invest in his family and to work on building a new relationship with them. His wife and children responded to his efforts and agreed to continue to work towards developing a healthy family relationship with each other.

If you love, live with, or lead a Lion, I have essential gifts for you in a later chapter. Now let's look at those Competent Camels.

CHAPTER FOUR

COMPETENT CAMELS

"Rule number one is, don't sweat the small stuff. Rule number two is, it's all small stuff."

—Robert Eliot

LITTLE TASKS

Competent Camels care much more about the process than the accomplishment. In other words, they are more concerned about how to get to the bottom line than actually getting to the bottom line. When you think of Camels, think of processors, organizers, or systemic thinkers. It's all in the details for Camels. They are naturally introverted and pride themselves on following the rules. Camels and Boy Scouts have the same motto: always be prepared. Spontaneity is not a friend of the Camel. Ms. Camel likes to have a plan, follow the plan, and complete the plan. Camels will have their act together and go to great lengths to make sure all the details have been covered. Camels love to make lists and follow outlines, so for our Camel friends reading this book, your section will be listed in outline format. Enjoy!

1. Communication

a. **Organization.** The Camel is what I call a go-to person. You can depend on Camels to be organized and to follow the rules. They enjoy the process of processing, and they love structure. Mr. Camel is a black and white thinker and therefore generally communicates in a very logical format.

b. **People skills**. People skills are not a strong suit of the thoroughbred Camel. They are not hardwired for casual, meaningless conversation, and need to have a purpose to their words. Otherwise why bother? Therefore, they may come across as somewhat straightforward or lacking in emotion.

c. **Communicating with Camels.** When communicating with a camel it is a good idea to take some time to organize your thoughts before speaking. For important conversations, prepare an agenda or create a structured format. This indicates to the Camel that you have invested time and thought into the issue at hand.

d. **Details.** With Camels, you can never have too much information . . . the more details the better.

2. Relationships

a. **External Expectations.** Camels tend to place high expectations on those with whom they are in a relationship. Many times these expectations are unreasonable and therefore unreachable. When those around Mr. Camel do not meet his unrealistic expectations, he may become critical or negative towards that person.

b. **Boundaries.** If you are in a relationship with someone who is a Camel, this next statement may be the most important thing you read in this book: You can never meet all of the expectations of the Camel. So stop trying! Instead, develop reasonable expectations that allow you to meet the needs of the Camels in your life. This requires setting appropriate boundaries. A boundary is defined as "a line that separates one thing from another." An emotional boundary means to draw a line or to separate reasonable expectations from unreasonable expectations. These boundaries or expectations are set by you as you invest in the relationship. For instance, the camel in your life may expect you to be organized in every area of your life. This is an unreasonable expectation that leads to frustration within the relationship. In a work environment, the camel may expect coworkers to perform with perfection. This is unreasonable and will lead to low morale and dysfunction on the team. It may sound strange, but helping the Camel to set reasonable expectations for a relationship is one of the best things you can do for him or her.

c. **Personal Expectations: The Pursuit of Perfection.** There is one person, however, on whom Mr. Camel places even higher expectations than those around him. That person is himself. Camels struggle with the "P" word: perfection. They set extremely high expectations on themselves. In other words, many times they set perfection as an expectation. Remember, the truth is that no one can achieve perfection all of the time. Therefore, the Camel's expectations for themselves become irrational. These unmet expectations tend to push the Camel into a downward spiral of frustration, guilt, and feelings of incompetency. Once on the downward spiral, the Camel may struggle with depression tendencies and/or negative thoughts and feelings. This mindset transitions into the critical nature they may bring into relationships. The old saying rings true: "If I don't like myself, then I generally do not like those around me."

d. **An Example of Camel Behavior:** Jessica the Camel is a student in high school and has just received a test back from one of her teachers. Jessica is horrified to see that there are two red marks of correction on her work and that she has only made a ninety-eight on the test! Jessica was sure she was going to receive a perfect score of one hundred when she took the test. She immediately goes to the teacher to protest her grade. "Please look at this again," she says, "I am sure that I should have received a score of one hundred on this test!" Meanwhile, in the back of the room, Jessica's friend Alicia, a Monkey, has just received her test back as well and is thinking, "Yeah! Life is fine with my seventy-nine!" Okay, this is an exaggeration, and I am not portraying all Monkeys as C students, but the point is that many times Camels are satisfied with nothing less than perfection.

e. **Another Example.** Zoe, the Camel and Jon, the Monkey, were engaged to be married. They had been dating for four months, and the wedding date was seven months away. Jon wanted to "forget all the wedding stuff" and "just run away and get married." While Zoe loved Jon, she had been thinking about, planning, and organizing her wedding since childhood. She knew what colors she wanted, what time of day the wedding would take place, where the ceremony would be conducted, what her wedding cake would look like, etc. Jon had never given any thought to those details, and quite frankly, couldn't care less about them.

When Zoe and Jon began to discuss this issue, other concerns about their relationship began to surface. Jon loved spontaneous experiences while Zoe loved the planning and anticipation of an event. While Jon would tell Zoe often how much he loved her and that she was "his beauty queen," he forgot simple details that were important to Zoe. For example, when they were ordering steak at a restaurant, he would never remember that she liked her steaks cooked medium well with a slightly pink middle. He rarely showed up on time for a date; in fact, he rarely planned a date before he arrived at her apartment. While these are small things, they represent why Zoe was beginning to feel disrespected and unloved. Likewise, Jon loved it when Zoe would "let her hair down and have fun" with him, but those times seemed to be few and far between. While she was always prompt and her life seemed to be organized, Jon loved just hanging out with no plan or agenda. While she was busy helping him clean his messy apartment, Jon just wanted to go to the park for a pizza picnic and clean later. Zoe told Jon occasionally that she loved him, but words of affirmation from her were sparse. This couple was experiencing the difficultly of a relationship with different personalities. The good news is that they discovered how to speak each other's personality language. This led to more self-awareness and increased understanding of one another. The good news for you is that we are going to talk about how to meet the needs of each personality trait later in this book!

3. PERCEPTION

a. **Myth #1: We judge others based on our own value system.** The Camel values competence, attention to details, follow-through, organization, following the rules, and working the plan. Along comes Mr. Monkey with little or no structure, just loving life and having fun. He wants to "seize the moment" and live life to its fullest. Consider Ms. Lion, who shows up already roaring, ready to accomplish the task and deal with the details later. "Let's make it happen!" is her cry. Along comes Mr. Turtle who needs some time to think about things. He wants to be sure the group is heading in the right direction and that they don't get too stressed out in the process. The Camel, when only looking through her own value lens, may see the Monkey as silly and obnoxious, the Lion as rude and having no clue about the details at hand, and the Turtle as unmotivated and lazy. The result is that these personalities will feel invalidated and therefore the Camel will not make a difference in their lives.

b. **Myth #2: Others view us the same way that we view ourselves.** The Camel views himself as someone who is dependable, logical, reliable, and prepared. Monkeys may view the Camel as boring, uptight, mean, and just plain anal. Lions may view the Camel as too worried about the little stuff, living in the weeds and not able to see the big picture. Turtles may see the Camel as too anxious, as not concerned about people but only the process, and possessing no ability to relax. So the question for the Camel is, "How do I make a difference in the lives of those whom I love, live with, and lead?"

c. **An example:** Katherine was at a crossroads with her career as well as in her life. She was a thoroughbred Camel and had worked her way up through hard work and a strong knowledge base to a position of leadership within her organization. The problem was that her leadership skills were centered only on her knowledge base of the product. Katherine was a great employee with exceptional talent, but when it came to leading people, she was ill-prepared for the job. The result was that her team was falling behind in productivity, efficiency was down, and absenteeism was up. Her employees frequently lamented the day the "wicked witch from the west" came into power. While Katherine's employees were cordial to her face, she knew that the team's morale was at an all-time low. The vice-president of operations gave Katherine sixty days to turn things around or she would be reassigned to an individual contributor position.

Katherine decided to seek the advice of an older, more experienced manager within the company. The manager replied, "You have the competence for this position, but you are leading others the way you want to be led. Katherine, you must choose to get to where your people are and learn to speak their language. That means you need to invest in people skills training, and expand your leadership toolbox with tools for effectively navigating those you lead." Katherine took his advice and began the process of learning to lead people instead of simply managing their tasks. Once she became aware that not everyone values organization and structure the way she does, she was able to learn the language of the other personality traits. Now, while she still does not "get" some of the Monkeys' jokes, she has developed strong relationships with her team based on their individual personality tendencies. The result is that she has a highly functioning team who recently nominated her for boss of the month within their organization. Katherine the Camel learned the secret of making a difference.

4. Stress

a. **An Example:** Now it's time to talk about how Camels generally handle stress. Remember our stressor for this example: our house is on fire. Ms. Camel is in her den reading a book entitled *Logistics as Related to Processes* when she realizes that her kitchen is in flames! She immediately begins to practice her fire drill plan that she developed in case of such an emergency. Ms. Camel calls 911 and wonders if she will be charged for this service. When the firefighters arrive, they find Ms Camel has pulled the garden hose into the kitchen and is spraying one small corner of the kitchen. She has become so focused on this corner that she does not realize that the entire kitchen is in flames. As the firemen rush in to fight the fire, Ms. Camel says, "I really don't need any help, I'm in the process of putting out the fire," and then because she feels she knows the problems and particulars of the fire in this one corner better than the new people on the scene, she utters that infamous Camel phrase, "I'll just do it myself."

b. **Micromanaging.** In times of stress, Camels tend to micromanage the situation. In doing so, they often frustrate those they are leading. This also causes the Camel to lose sight of the big picture. Ms. Camel, remember that it is important to allow others to help you in times of stress. They may not resolve the issue just the way you would, but the process will build stronger and more fulfilling relationships with those you care about.

c. **Another Example.** Here's another example concerning how Camels deal with stress. Let's look back at Katherine who sought advice from a more experienced manager within her company. That experienced manager's name is Mr. Blyth. Mr. Blyth is in his mid-fifties, married, with two adult children. He received his accounting degree from a state university and began his career with the corporation Widget Tech as a staff accountant. As with all young graduates, Mr. Blyth wanted to impress his boss early on, so he went about demonstrating an exemplary work ethic including timeliness to the office, quality of work, and a particular eye for detail. His strategy paid off, and within three years Mr. Blyth was promoted to senior accountant within his company. As is common in the corporate world, Widget Tech was eventually purchased by a larger corporation, and Mr. Blyth found himself in a sea of uncertainty and anonymity. However, Mr. Blyth kept his "head down" and continued his routine of doing his job effectively and efficiently. Another two years went by, and Mr. Blyth became aware that although he was a hard worker, and respected in his own department, the opportunity for advancement into the management level of the company seemed dim. In fact, it appeared that while his supervisor appreciated his eye for detail and his desire to complete tasks with great proficiency, when leadership or manager decisions were to be made, his supervisor regularly conferred with others within the department. Besides that, while Mr. Blyth had a cordial relationship with those around him, he considered investing in any kind of relationship as unprofessional and quite frankly a waste of time. Therefore, his daily routine was as follows: get to work a minimum of fifteen minutes early, grab a hot cup of coffee, then go to his cubicle. Once in his cubicle he began his work. Mr. Blyth worked steadily until his break, which he generally took by himself. After that he worked until lunch, which he observed either at his desk or alone. At the end of the day Mr. Blyth would make sure that his work area was neat, clean, and tidy then he would leave, once again alone. He did not reach out to those around him to enrich his corporate experience.

Because of this, Mr. Blyth had a growing sense of being trapped in the corporate sea of ambiguity. Each day bled into the next. Mr. Blyth began to look elsewhere for job opportunities. It was no surprise when he turned in his resignation to Widget Tech to begin another opportunity with Product Co., which was somewhat smaller but had high growth opportunity. The turning point in his career, however, was not when Mr. Blyth changed companies but when he had a strategic conversation with his wife. Being a Camel, Mr. Blyth wanted to analyze exactly what those seven years working for Widget Tech had produced.

On the Friday evening before he was to begin work at his new company, Mr. Blyth was talking with his wife and said, "You know, I just can't understand why I was not promoted within my old company. I've analyzed every angle; my work ethic was extremely strong, I always arrived to work early, I always stayed if needed to complete a task, I never complained; I just kept my head down and did my work. I've been taught all my life that hard work will lead you to promotions within an organization. I was organized, efficient, detail-driven, and yet I sat virtually in the same spot of the corporate ladder for the last seven years. I just don't understand it."

His wife responded, "It's true that you are a very hard worker and give much attention to detail and to completing the task correctly. However, I have observed that throughout your entire career up to this point, you have developed very few significant relationships outside our home. In other words, while you are invested in your task, it appears to me that you have not invested in professional relationships. As I have observed other people, it appears to me that there is more to climbing the corporate ladder than simply working hard. If you desire to lead others you might want to consider investing in the 'people side' of your job."

While Mr. Blyth did not exactly understand all that his wife was trying to communicate, he did comprehend that he had not developed any significant professional or business relationships. That's when Mr. Blyth made a commitment to begin the journey of learning how to lead people, not just tasks. He first invested in several books that addressed the issue of relationships and leading (much like the one you are reading at this moment). He also committed to spending his own resources if necessary to gain knowledge to learn the people side of his occupation. The result was that through the years with Product Co., Mr. Blyth, through books, seminars, conferences and one-on-one coaching, gained an awareness of how to lead others in an effective manner. As he told Katherine many years later, he chose to get where his people are, and he learned to speak their language. The transformation that Mr. Blyth experienced resulted not only in upward movement through the corporate ladder, but in an awareness that he had the ability to make a difference in the lives of others. Interestingly enough, through the years of his career, Mr. Blyth became known as less of an accountant and more as an experienced mentor and leader who truly cared about others.

If you love, live with, or lead a camel, I have essential gifts for you in a later chapter. But for now let's look at those Tranquil Turtles.

CHAPTER FIVE

TRANQUIL TURTLES

"The difference between a smart man and a wise man is that a smart man knows what to say, a wise man knows whether or not to say it."

—Frank M. Garafola

PERSON ORIENTED

Tranquil Turtles place an incredible amount of importance on one-on-one interpersonal relationships. They are **person oriented**. Whether personal or business, Turtles bring perspective to the relationship. They are intensely **loyal** and have the ability to bring much **wisdom** to a given situation. Remember the old commercial that promoted, "When E. F. Hutton speaks—people listen"? When the Tranquil Turtle speaks it is important to listen, for the Turtle's wisdom can save time, money, and increase productivity in a business. In relationships, that wisdom can prove to be vital in establishing perspective and understanding. Turtles are extremely flexible and tend to be **low maintenance**. Mr. Turtle is a man of few words. So for our Turtle friends who are reading about themselves in this book, please note that the most important words of each section are in bold.

COMMUNICATION

Even though the Turtle is an introvert by nature, he can be a powerful communicator. However, if Ms. Turtle is not self-aware, her communication skills can be quite frustrating for those around her. **Turtles excel with one-on-one communication, but they struggle with mass communication, or communicating spontaneously to groups of people.** Even in a one-on-one setting the Turtle must have an appropriate amount of time to process his or her thoughts before speaking. Turtles are great listeners. They tend to be aware of other peoples' emotions, behaviors, and thought processes. The intrinsic nature of the Turtle generally allows him or her to have a very powerful and illusive "poker face" when it comes to displaying emotions. **When communicating with a Turtle, it is important to remember to slow down and allow them to have some processing time.** This looks like: communicating several issues that are of significant importance with Mr. Turtle, giving him time to process these issues, and defining a timeline or a deadline by which you need his response.

To extroverted Monkeys and Lions, waiting for the Turtle to process and get back to them can be painful. But remember, everyone has his or her own neurological chemistry, so learning to communicate with the Turtle in ways which he or she can receive that communication will not only benefit the Turtle, but will also benefit those who take the time to invest in relationships with the Turtle.

Now I am fully aware that there are times when this methodology will not work. When that occurs, simply communicate your predicament up front when communicating with the Turtle, ask him or her to join you in some quick decision making or thought processing. While this is not a comfortable place for the Turtle to be, he or she can certainly engage in this type of communication if parameters are set ahead of time. A caution here is that if you overuse the "crisis communication" model with a Turtle, you will lose the credibility with that individual. Operating out of a sense of urgency is not a strength of Turtles, so overusing a sense of urgency to push a Turtle to decide or communicate causes frustration, and eventually it will have the opposite effect: the Turtle will actually slow down the decision-making process if he is continually bombarded with urgent situations that are not actual emergencies or crises.

RELATIONSHIPS

Strong relationships are vital to the well-being of Turtles. While they do not desire a vast number of relationships, they intensely yearn for just a few, very deep relationships.

Let's take a step back here and take a look at the relationship model which will help us to understand the depth of a Turtle's one-on-one relationships. Think of a bull's-eye with five rings. Number those rings one to five with one being the smallest ring at the center of the bull's-eye. Two is the next largest ring, followed by rings three, four and five, ending with five being the largest outer ring of the bull's-eye. Each of these rings represents a relationship level.

Relationship Level Five—This level represents our acquaintances. **Acquaintances are the people that we may recognize, and we may even remember their names, but we have very little in common with them and have relatively no investment in their lives.** It is with this relationship that we all participate in "the great American lie." When we see a Level Five relationship individual we generally ask, "How are you?" to which they generally lie and say, "I'm fine. How are you?" to which we generally lie back and say, "I'm fine too, thanks." The truth is that it really doesn't matter if we are *fine* or not; we are going to say we are "fine" because it is the accepted greeting within our culture for acquaintances, whereas if we were with people we hold closer to us, we might reveal how we are truly feeling and what is going on in our lives. The large size of this ring represents that we have many such acquaintances in our lives.

Relationship Level Four—This level represents those people we call our *friends*. These are the people that we may go to church with; they may be our neighbors or our coworkers. We know their names. We may even know something about their families. **With our friends we may have casual conversations that generally last two to three minutes in which we engage in surface talk about things that are going on in our lives.** These relationships are nonthreatening, generic, and comfortable.

Relationship Level Three—This level represents the *close friends* in our life. **These are friends with whom we have invested an amount of time, energy, and resources. We have developed a large knowledge of information about these close friends.** We enjoy communicating and being with these friends on a regular basis. We know that should we have a crisis in our families, or a need, we could count on our close friends to respond to that need on both physical and emotional levels, and we would do the same for them. However, there are things that are kept from these close friends that are just "too private" to share. While we connect with our close friends in many ways, we do not connect with them on every level of our lives. To help define a close friends' relationship level, think of friends you are comfortable being with in a small group—for example, friends in a book club, dinner club, or small group study.

Relationship Level Two—This level represents our *best friends*. **Our best friends are those very few individuals (notice that the level two ring is much smaller than the level five ring) whom we trust and with whom we have invested an enormous amount of time, energy, and even resources**. These individuals are the ones you would go to should you face an intense crisis in your life. For example, this level two individual would be the one who walks with you through a divorce from your spouse or through an acute or chronic illness of yourself or a loved one. This individual would not only support you emotionally but would be there for you physically as well. These individuals are the ones that we feel comfortable traveling with on an extended vacation or spending significant amounts of time with on a regular basis. We trust them on a very deep level and many times consider them "family." With these individuals we can be ourselves and know that we will not be judged based on our appearances or our status. Because of the depth of our investment and the time and energy it takes, we only have a few best friends in our lives.

Relationship Level One—This level represents the *intimate friends* in our lives. **Generally this is one person or possibly two people with whom we would trust our very souls.** This person is the one with whom we can be emotionally naked. We realize that this person knows everything about us—the good, the bad, and the ugly. We know that we could commit the most heinous crime, and while this person may not condone our behavior, he or she would still love us unconditionally. This person unequivocally knows us better than anyone else on the planet. He or she places no judgment on us, and accepts us totally. While this person may not always agree with us or even like us, this person will always love us. The depth of this intimate relationship cannot adequately be described with words. If you are fortunate enough to experience level one friendships, you understand the depth of vulnerability, trust, and love that this level represents.

In considering the five relationship levels, Turtles place much more importance on developing levels one and two relationships. They are generally not interested in level four and level five relationships; they spend an exorbitant amount of time on level two and three relationships. However, their level three relationship circle will generally be smaller than the circles of other personalities, especially the extroverted personalities. Let's explain it this way: Turtles have few very deep, very personal friends. They operate out of the level one, two, and three relationship levels most of the time. It would be wise to remember that Turtles make exceptional best friends. Also remember that on a professional level, developing a relationship with a Turtle is essential to that business.

Allow me to give you an example. I serve as the executive coach for an individual who leads a mega-organization. He has responsibilities for over ten thousand employees. Interestingly, this individual's primary personality is Tranquil Turtle. His secondary personality is Leading Lion. For the purpose of this illustration we will call him Charley. As I worked with Charley I began to realize that he was a man of incredible intelligence, insight, and intellect. One of the great perks I have in my profession is the opportunity to observe and gain nuggets of wisdom from individuals such as Charley. As we began to walk on our journey together, I realized that I was going to have to earn the right to speak into Charley's life. In other words, I was going to have to invest in our relationship in order to connect with him on a significant level. It is interesting to note that I was introduced to Charley by someone he greatly admired and trusted and with whom he had developed a relationship. It was an honor to be brought into Charley's relationship circle, and I knew that this was going to be an experience like none other I had ever had.

I soon discovered that Charley had the incredible ability of accurately assessing the leadership and technical skills of others and placing them in the correct positions within the company in an almost flawless manner. This skill had propelled him to the highest level of his organization. Charley was literally entrusted with the lives of thousands of individuals. He was recognized nationally as an expert in his field, and was in high demand at many venues. Through my executive coaching relationship with Charley, we became close friends. Knowing how important relationships are to him, I count it an honor that he would choose to invest in our friendship on such a deep level. I also have benefited much from the insight and wisdom gained from my friend Charley. This just goes to show that there is much to be learned if a Turtle ever decides to bring you into his or her inner levels. Getting to level one or two with a Turtle takes a lot of work, energy, and investment, but once there you will find great rewards.

DECISION-MAKING

As we have stated previously, the Turtle is person oriented in relationships, and process oriented in decisions. He needs time to make a wise decision. However, when overusing his strength of wise decision making, the Turtle becomes a procrastinator. Turtles may have a tendency to overthink the situation, therefore delaying the decision-making process. Turtles desire to make the wisest decision, but carefully considering each aspect of the situation may result in little action actually being taken. Unmade decisions may result in the frustration and demoralization of those around Turtles, including those they lead. While the Turtle may be content to "stay and play in his own little mudhole," others do not share that contentment and need for the Turtle to develop a sense of urgency and make a decision. **It is important for Miss Turtle to be aware that even though she may not have an actual preference in a decision that is to be made, if it is her decision to make, she must move forward and choose an option.** This is less about what she desires and more about finding a definitive answer about an issue for those who do not share her Turtle contentment with the status quo.

PERCEPTION

Myth #1: We place value on others based on our value system. The Turtle places value on humility, working together, and a peaceful environment. Mr. Monkey comes along swinging from tree to tree with no structure and in a constant state of chaos. He is excited and wants to live for the moment. He seeks highly energized environments and loves to verbally problem-solve and brainstorm. This may frustrate the Turtle and cause the Turtle to invalidate the Monkey.

The Camel meanwhile seeks structure, rules, and organization. The Turtle may view the Camel as overly concerned about insignificant details. He may assume that the Camel cannot think philosophically or with grace, and he may become frustrated with the Camel because of the Camel's need for definitive timelines and action items. Therefore, the Turtle may invalidate the Camel in a personal or professional relationship.

The louder the Lion roars the less impressed the Turtle becomes. The Lion's big picture mentality and dominating aggressive personality will cause the Turtle to write Mr. Lion off as a self-centered noncontributory; thus the Turtle will invalidate Mr. Lion.

The net result of the Turtle's leading and investing in relationships only from his value system leads to the invalidation of the other three personalities; therefore, the Turtle will not make a difference in their lives.

Myth 2: Others view us the same way that we view ourselves. The Turtle views himself as a peacemaker, as one who has the ability to assess the situation and deliver a wise decision with calmness and steadiness. The Turtle views himself as one with insight and depth. Contrary to that, the Monkey may view the Turtle as one who is disconnected from others on a surface level. From her Monkey perspective, she may see the Turtle as unapproachable, hard to reach, and distant.

Mr. Camel may view the Turtle as one who has a difficult time with follow-through, and who does not pay attention to the given set of standards and rules that pertain to a decision. Mr. Camel may view the Turtle as too dependent on relationships and therefore believe that the Turtle may not be able to make logical and rational decisions.

The Lion may see the Turtle as slow, weak, and wishy-washy. The Lion's need for a dominant and impulsive type of decision will generally be unmet by the Turtle; therefore, the Lion assumes that the Turtle has little ability to lead and less ability to make important and swift decisions. The Lion assumes that a slow decision equals no decision.

If the Turtle is to make a difference in the lives of those she lives with, leads, or loves, she will have to choose to address both Myth 1 as well as Myth 2.

ADDRESSING THE MYTHS

Addressing both Myth 1 and Myth 2 for Turtles involves learning how to validate the values of the other three personalities as well as developing a sense of awareness of how those personalities may perceive the Turtle.

Allow me to refer to our previous example of Charley, the executive in charge of a mega-organization. I have had the opportunity to observe how Charley leads various leaders within his organization who have different and varied personalities. I was once invited to a major public relations event where Charley was to be the keynote speaker. I was amazed as this Turtle "worked the room" prior to his speech. He was enthusiastic, positive, and presented his speech with a tremendous amount of people skills. I watched as this introverted Turtle "slapped backs," "shook hands," and created a sense of excitement and anticipation for his vision.

I watched as Charley presented an incredible speech that set the tone for this multi-million dollar organization and defined objective long-range vision, as well as short and midterm action items that would set the course of direction for the years to come. Later as I was meeting with Charley individually, I asked him about that event. "How did you become such a Monkey?" I asked. Charley smiled and said, "Because I care about the people of this organization, and because many have worked hard to create and implement the vision for this organization, I became who I needed to be in order to connect with the people in the room."

I have also observed Charley demonstrate the value system of the Monkey as he led one of his vice-presidents. This particular individual, while possessing an incredible intellect, also carried much insecurity. Charley offered security to his vice-president by connecting with a shared laugh or words of encouragement.

I also observed as Charley led another one of his vice-presidents, a thoroughbred Camel. She was a genius with organization and structure. Her competency in her given job assignment was invaluable to Charley as well as to the organization. However, when major changes approached the scene, or when the structure had to be flexed, she needed to be guided through her frustrations with the changes. I watched as Charley navigated her successfully through the changes. Charley was always specific when leading this vice-president, and surrounded each conversation with precise outlines, action items, and expectations.

Charley taught me that regardless of our own personalities, it is our responsibility to learn how to connect effectively with those around us. This is true professionally and emotionally.

STRESS

Let's turn our attention now to learning how a Turtle generally handles stress. Remember our stressor: your house is burning. Mr. Turtle, of course, is asleep on his sofa alone in the den when the kitchen bursts into flames. Mr. Turtle arises from his nap and notices there is some smoke in the room, but in true Turtle fashion says, "I wonder what that smoke is? Maybe I'll find out later . . . Maybe it will just go away." He then resumes his nap only to be awakened a few minutes later by his den filled with smoke.

At this point the Turtle begins to think about his options. He wonders if he should call 911 or perhaps try to put the flames out himself. Another option would be to go to the neighbors' house and see if they are home and perhaps ask if they could help with this problem. He wonders how much damage the fire is really going to do to his home anyway, and is it worth the effort to try to extinguish the fire immediately, or could he put it off and get back to it in the near future?

Fast forward an hour or so, and the Turtle has now pulled his sofa into the front yard, where he sits and watches his house burning, completely engulfed in flames. "Just look at that thing burn; you know I really do need to call someone," he says to himself.

This is an obvious exaggeration of how a Turtle deals with stress, but the point is that in times of stress Turtles tend to deny and withdraw. **The Turtle will go into his shell in times of acute crisis. When the urgency of the situation speeds up the Turtle tends to slow down in his decision-making process**. This lack of urgency or inability to make a timely decision can result in the degeneration or demoralization of a team or a relationship.

Consider this example: Caroline was a high-energy Lion who had just been given the award of Small Business of the Year from her local Chamber of Commerce. Her consulting business centered upon her ability to deliver sound marketing and sale strategies for her clients. Because of the growth of her business Sandra hired Peter, a thoroughbred Turtle, to help with the graphic design and marketing materials needed for her clients.

Peter and Caroline worked together for approximately eight months when their relationship began going downhill fast. Caroline relied on deadlines that had to be met in order for her to meet the needs of her clients. She was awarded the Small Business of the Year because of her ability to provide a quality product in a timely manner and also because of her integrity in keeping her word and delivering on the promises that she made to her clients. Peter, on the other hand, was committed to providing an excellent product graphically. This, he reasoned, took time to make sure that the client's needs were thoroughly defined, developed, and covered in the graphic materials.

As Caroline's clientele grew in number, the demand on Peter grew as well. The harder Caroline seemed to push Peter, the slower Peter delivered his marketing materials. As you can imagine, this story was heading for a tragic ending. However, Caroline and Peter both chose to invest in the process of learning about relationships and choosing to make a difference in the lives of those around them. The result was that Caroline began to lead Peter by providing deadlines and priority lists. Peter understood that as a Lion, Caroline lived from crisis to crisis. Consequently, he began to help her differentiate between the projects that were urgent and those projects that were not urgent. Together they began to recognize each other's strengths and weaknesses.

Today Caroline's business continues to flourish and she counts Peter as a vital member of her leadership team. Later you will be given very powerful essential gifts for those who love, live with, or lead Turtles, but for now, on to the next chapter.

CHAPTER SIX

COMMITMENT TO CONFLICT

"Whenever you're in conflict with someone, there is one factor that can make the difference between damaging your relationship and deepening it. That factor is attitude."
—William James

CONFLICT IS NECESSARY

One of the key ingredients to successfully navigating relationships is healthy conflict. Generally, when we think of conflict it brings a negative connotation to our minds. That is, we have negative mental pictures associated with the word "conflict." However, all healthy teams and all healthy relationships must have conflict. **Believe it or not, conflict is a good thing.** It gives us the ability to authentically share our feelings, provide input from different perspectives, and create ownership and accountability.

Let me take this conflict thing a step further: **If your relationship does not have conflict, then it is not a healthy relationship.** Likewise, if a team does not have conflict it is not a progressive, growing, productive team. Let's start with a definition of conflict: conflict is defined as "a disagreement that occurs in groups or in relationships when differences regarding ideas, methods, and individuals are expressed" (WISINSKI, 1993).

When conflict arises an unhealthy cycle may begin. Many people don't understand the value of conflict or the personalities of others on their team or in their relationships. Therefore, conflict is not settled in a healthy manner. The result is a mess where everyone leaves frustrated and wounded by the unhealthy confrontation. Understandably, sometimes people within relationships come to feel that their relationships are not worth going into a confrontational battle anymore. An unspoken truce is developed. The frustrations and disagreements are still there, but they are not spoken out loud. In the counseling arena this is called denial, or even disassociation, from the truth. This generally leads to what counselors call passive/aggressive or avoidant behavior. The result of this unspoken conflict is anger that is never communicated and continues to grow. Before we take a look at how each personality type tends to deal with conflict, let's take a look at anger.

ANGER

Many times anger is associated with conflict. It seems to be that this is the default emotion for many people who enter into a conflict situation. When anger is expressed it is a sure bet that there is something lying beneath that anger. Conflict does not equal anger. Anger is a lashing-out response programmed into us as a defense mechanism; it indicates there is something wrong which needs to be fixed. Expressions of anger are merely a symptom that there is a deeper issue driving our behavior.

An example: Remember the last time you stubbed your toe or hurt yourself in a similar way. What did you feel, both physically and emotionally? Physically, I'm sure you felt pain; your toe hurt! Emotionally, I'm sure your body responded to that pain with its fight or flight instinct; in preparation of a fight response, it made you angry. Perhaps you yelled at your kids for leaving something of theirs in the way that caused you to trip on it. Perhaps you yelled at the object you tripped over, or even yourself. Your body's natural response to something being wrong was to get angry. In this situation, the anger wasn't the *problem*, but a *symptom* of your pain.

In relationships anger can work like this: Whenever an emotion or series of emotions occur, many people download this same emotional response file over and over again. They default to the anger mechanism. While they have the ability to download an infinite number of emotional responses to address the situations they encounter, many choose only to download anger. There are many reasons for this, and it would take writing another book to discover why some people default to the anger mechanism. But for our purposes, allow me to overgeneralize the main reason that someone may default to anger on a consistent basis in a relationship:

Reason One: Hurt. Hurt brings about loss and pain. We experience hurt when we lose something or someone that is important to us. We may experience hurt from the loss of a healthy child environment. We may experience hurt from rejection that we have felt from others. Hurt occurs when we have been emotionally wounded by someone or something. There are many ways that one may feel hurt or personal pain. Many times the easiest thing to do is to download anger as the body's natural defense to fix a situation, when what we are actually experiencing is hurt.

Reason Two: Disappointment. We all have expectations that we have set for ourselves, our families, our teams, and our relationships. When these expectations are unmet, disappointment may occur, but some people have a tendency to default to anger. Disappointment may occur when a marriage does not meet the expectations with which it was entered. Disappointment may occur because of the behavior of our children or our teammates at work. We may experience disappointment within ourselves because of our inability to be at a station in life where we expected to be at a given time. Life takes many unexpected twists and turns.

This unpredictable journey deals us disappointments, grief, and heartache. It is important for us to understand that many times when we download anger, what we are actually experiencing is disappointment in some form.

Reason Three: Vulnerability. The feeling of having been betrayed or taken advantage of on a deep level hits us in the core of our being and produces an instinctive response which many times can be one of overwhelming anger. Once we choose to be vulnerable, to expose our very souls and our deepest thoughts and desires, only to realize that the persons we trusted have betrayed us, we experience an intense feeling of misused vulnerability. The level of vulnerability may vary from relationship to relationship (remember the relationship levels and the bull's-eye). For instance, a marriage relationship would create more vulnerability than a business or team relationship. However, even professional relationships produce a level of vulnerability to those with which you engage or interact. In other words, for a team to be successful there must be a level of vulnerability or trust that each member will carry his or her own weight. Without the dynamic of vulnerability there can be no productivity within an organization, team, or relationship.

Allow me to note here that just as someone may use anger to respond to their breech of vulnerability, others may use anger to breech the vulnerability of those around them. Let me explain. Steve is a midlevel supervisor for a local distributing company. He supervises a team of fourteen men and women to provide inside sales for the company. Steve believes that "the only reason these people are here are to hit the numbers. It's a numbers game. We pay these people to come to work, and we expect them to work while they are here and focus on one thing—hitting their numbers." Steve greets each of his employees with intimidation, sarcasm, and dominance. Instead of effectively coaching an individual through a difficult sales period, Steve uses anger to "motivate" that individual. Steve calls it "being driven" and "focused." The result of Steve's angry response to his employees is a miserable work environment and high turnover among the inside sales team.

If you find yourself constantly downloading anger as your emotional response to hurt, disappointment, or vulnerability, I encourage you to see professional help with diagnosing the cause of this default emotion and working to improve. Great strides can be made with an individual who is committed to overcoming the dysfunctional response of an excessive use of anger. The truth is that all of us misuse anger from time to time. Becoming aware of what causes the anger may help us to take control of our own emotional responses and our own behaviors and will guide us effectively in conflict resolution.

Let's take a look at how each of the four personalities generally responds to conflict.

MUCH-LOVED MONKEYS

I nicknamed Monkeys as "much-loved" because that is exactly what they desire. Monkeys desire to love everyone and for everyone to love them. However, don't assume that because Monkeys love to be loved that they cannot produce intense anger. Most Monkeys, because of their extroverted nature, have the capability of displaying a nasty temper. Generally, a temper trigger for the Monkey is when someone they care about is being taken advantage of, or when Monkeys themselves feel they are being taken advantage of.

Monkeys may not get upset over the task, but they will get upset for the person. When Monkeys get angry their anger is expressed in a very verbal, emotion-based way and can become irrational. Monkeys' anger seems to be spontaneous and short-lived. Monkeys do not like the feeling of anger; therefore, they do not allow themselves to stay angry for a very long period. Monkeys may be quick to say "I'm sorry" after a conflict, and they have a wonderful ability to easily offer forgiveness to others. They generally do not hold grudges, and work to provide harmony in relationships. During a time of conflict the Monkey desires first to be heard, and secondly to restore the relationship. Many times the resolution of the problem is not as important to the Monkey as the resolution of the relationship. Therefore, Monkeys can more easily agree to disagree about the actual problem as long as the relationship can be restored. So when in conflict with a Monkey, remember to allow them to verbalize their feelings, thoughts and emotions, keeping in mind that some of their verbalization may be emotion-based and therefore irrational. Offer security in the relationship then address the conflict issue. When all else fails, agree to disagree.

LEADING LION

Most Lions are natural-born fighters. They love the challenge of overcoming a difficult situation. They see conflict as "going into battle." In their minds there are only two options when entering into a battle: win or lose—and the Lion is determined to win. In fact, thoroughbred Lions will seek out conflict if things become too comfortable in their environment.

In times of conflict Lions become passionate about the issue. To Lions, the most important item at hand is to win the battle. Lions have their eyes on the big picture of winning, many times at the expense of their relationships. I have observed Lions in the middle of monumental conflict; they vow to resolve the issue in the fastest and "best" way they see fit. They accomplish the task and "fix" the problem. However, at the end of the day when they look back, it becomes clear that the Lions have left a trail of severed relationships and hurt people in the wake of their roaring solutions to the problems at hand.

Lions love to lead and have no problem leading the charge in a conflict situation. Therefore, when entering into a conflict with a Lion, it is important to remember that Lions use words as tools in a conflict, or as a way to win the battle. Therefore, do not take anything the Lion says when in a conflict situation too personally. Lions respect strength, so when in a conflict stay in control and use strong language (I'm not talking about the R-rated strong language), such as: "I can; I will; You will; You will not; and We will" versus "We could; We might; We should, etc." Once the conflict has been resolved the Lion has no problem moving on to the next task at hand. They will only look forward to the next conflict to win. It is helpful to frame conflict with a Lion so that opportunities are presented for creative conflict resolution strategies versus "all or none" or "win or lose" conflict resolution strategies.

COMPETENT CAMEL

Camels are intense rule followers. Most conflicts with Camels arise because someone has broken the rules. Camels live in a black and white world. Therefore, to a Camel, conflict looks black or white, right or wrong. There is very little gray area. When a Camel's expectations are unmet, this can produce anger and frustration which leads to conflict.

Anger for Camels tends to be triggered by a lack of accountability, or lack of follow-through on assigned tasks. Camels take the words of others very literally. In other words, if you say you are going to do something, Camels will be very hurt if you do not follow through with your promise.

Camels are literal thinkers. They are also naturally introverted, so Mr. Camel may hold his anger or frustration inside at first. However, if given the opportunity, or put in the appropriate environment, Mr. Camel will share his thoughts on the conflict situation. Keep in mind that Mr. Camel is logic driven, so he will verbalize what he considers to be accurate, precise, and true thoughts on the issue at hand. If you remember the old Star Trek series, Mr. Spock is a good example of a thoroughbred Camel. In a conflict conversation, Camels will win their case with data and a multitude of details. Mr. Camel cares much about the specifics of the conflict versus the philosophy of the conflict. So when entering into a conflict conversation with a Camel, remember, it's all about the details. Allow the Camel to be heard.

Listening to Camels looks like the following: Allow the Camel to present their detailed outline analysis of why they believe that they are correct in this situation. Stay away from vague language with a Camel. Try to enter into a conflict conversation that is surrounded in accuracy and logic. Remember, the Camel is concerned about correct procedures being followed and that justice is accomplished. Emotional connection is not the top priority of the camel.

TRANQUIL TURTLE

Much like Monkeys, Turtles disdain conflict. However, while Mr. Monkey attempts to please everyone and create harmony, Ms. Turtle will hold her feelings inside. Turtles are introverts, which mean they hold their cards very close to their chests. They may feel strongly about an issue and yet never verbalize their thoughts. Turtles generally deal with conflict in a very passive manner. While their strength in conflict situations is not allowing the small areas of conflict to distract or concern them, their weakness lies in not addressing the major issues that arise in a conflict conversation.

Tranquil Turtles are masters at avoiding verbal confrontations. While it's true that it takes a lot to anger a thoroughbred Turtle, once that point is reached it is equally difficult for a Turtle to let go of his or her deep-seated hurt, anger, or frustration. When dealing with a Turtle in a conflict situation, remember that your first objective is to create a safe environment for a Turtle to verbalize his or her true feelings on the matter. The process of conflict resolution with a Turtle is slow and might even include periods of silence. This will be especially frustrating for extroverted Monkeys or Lions. Turtles need time to process the situation and to articulate their opinions and feelings. Most of the time, Mr. Turtle will choose his words very carefully. The result is when the Turtle speaks he generally means what he says. The conflict resolution process is painful for Turtles, and therefore they may avoid the process for as long as possible.

Additionally, be careful not to fall into the "Turtle Tapper" methodology when resolving conflict with a Turtle. The Turtle Tapper approach looks like this: Gina, a Monkey/Lion personality, has a conflict to resolve with Keith the Turtle. Giving in to her impulsivity, Gina decides that they need to resolve the conflict as quickly as possible, dealing with it right now, and then moving on immediately. "Keith" she says, "We need to talk. I totally disagree with the way you handled that situation earlier, and we need to resolve it immediately."

Keith is in the middle of his Turtle time and prefers not to be disturbed at the moment, but Gina persists and begins to barrage Keith with a verbal assault on why he was wrong in the given situation. This causes Keith to withdraw from the conversation and eventually from Gina's presence. This infuriates Gina, so she follows him from room to room, demanding that he stop avoiding her and resolve this conflict immediately! Gina's insistence and aggression only cause Keith to be more passive and more determined not to have a conversation with her. The result is that the conflict is nowhere near being resolved, and the emotional separation of Gina and Keith has actually become greater.

Gina chose to pick up her Turtle Tapper to resolve this conflict. As she approached Keith she began by taking her Turtle Tapper and tapping it on Keith the Turtle's shell. This of course caused Keith to do what all Turtles do—to go inside his shell. Thinking that she needed to take control of the situation, Gina tapped harder on the shell. The harder Gina tapped, the more determined Keith became not to stick his head out of his shell.

Obviously the Turtle Tapping had an adverse effect on resolving the conflict at hand. Had Gina chosen to put the Turtle Tapper down, and instead of tapping on Keith's shell chosen to perhaps rub his Turtle tummy, that would have encouraged Keith to engage in the conflict conversation in a safe environment. Rubbing the Turtle's tummy (you can giggle if you want) looks like this:

Gina approaches Keith in a very calm manner and says, "Keith, I believe we had a misunderstanding concerning that situation earlier, and I would like for us to set a time to discuss this when you are ready." Keith would have responded that he needed some personal reflection time right now, and that he would be glad to discuss their conflict at a later time. When he says this, Gina could gently push the issue and say, "Let's set a time so that we don't procrastinate on resolving this conflict, because it is very important to me, and I believe it's important to our relationship as well," and then Gina and Keith would agree upon a set time to discuss their conflict.

When they eventually meet to discuss their issues, the conflict will have a much greater chance of being resolved in a healthy manner than if Gina had ignored Keith's emotional needs as a Turtle.

Let's look at some general areas of conflict that may consistently arise when attempting to resolve an issue for any animal personality. Dr. John Gottman, at the University of Washington, has developed what he calls the Four Horsemen of the Relationship Apocalypse. I will list the four horsemen in the order of which I generally observe an unhealthy conflict pattern progressing.

HORSEMAN #1: CRITICISM

In a relationship or on a team, this tends to be the most common horseman seen. Unmet expectations, annoyances, and frustrations arise in relationships. These can be manifested in criticism towards one another, especially in the heat of an argument. Dr. Gottman substantiates that he believes most conflict situations begin with criticism within a relationship. He recommends changing your approach from criticism to complaining. Dr. Gottman states that criticism is different than complaining. Criticism focuses on the person and complaining focuses on the behavior.

While the difference between criticism and complaining may seem insignificant, research indicates that this distinction actually makes a significant difference in the long-term health of a relationship. You separate criticism from complaining by choosing to use the appropriate prefix in conversation. For example, a critical statement might be, "You always leave the toilet lid up. You are inconsiderate and messy." These are words that lead to blame and accusation. They feel like a personal attack. Complaining deals more with how you feel about the behavior of the other person. Complaining usually begins with an "I" instead of "You." So, the revised statement would be, "I get so frustrated when you leave the toilet lid up and I have to continually close it myself." The difference is that the second statement speaks negatively about the behavior versus language that would indicate a personal attack. Using "I" statements may seem awkward at first, but once practiced they can really help to direct the tone of a conflict.

HORSEMAN #2: DEFENSIVENESS

Once criticism occurs, the natural response is to become defensive. This is a natural coping mechanism or strategy for dealing with criticism. In fact, it may even be an involuntary reflex in a relationship or team where criticism is constant and affirmation comes seldom. At its fundamental roots, defensiveness is a self-preservation tactic from an emotional standpoint. Remember the example of stubbing your toe? Whereas anger is a reaction to pain, defensiveness is a reaction to criticism. As understandable as this is, defensiveness continues the dysfunctional spiral of unhealthy conflict resolution. It allows walls to be built, disconnection to occur, and creates emotional distance within the relationship. The result is that defensiveness blocks open communication and authentic resolution of conflict.

In order for one not to be defensive, one must make a conscious, intentional choice not to respond in this manner. This choice is difficult, at best. Unless a person is self-aware at all times, he or she may slip into the pattern of defensiveness. One way defensiveness shows itself is in excuse making. When you find yourself making excuses for the criticism versus finding a true solution to the criticism, you may be responding out of the second horseman of defensiveness.

HORSEMAN #3: STONE-WALLING

This generally occurs after the criticism has continued and the defensiveness has become a regular coping mechanism. Stone-Walling happens when one or both parties feel overwhelmed with the conflict and therefore withdraw verbally, emotionally, and/or physically from the situation, or in extreme cases, from the relationship itself. Stone-walling manifests itself with faceless expressions, eye contact avoidance, rigid posture, inactive listening, and no verbal feedback. It is used to radiate an icy polarization that signals disapproval to others in the relationship or on the team. While Stone-Walling is not directly aggressive, it is passively aggressive and incredibly destructive. It can devastate the relationship and close the door to any possibility of a healthy resolution. Choosing not to succumb to stone-walling means choosing to actively engage in the conversation regardless of how difficult it becomes. This means choosing to respond verbally and nonverbally in a conflict conversation.

HORSEMAN #4: CONTEMPT

Dr. Gottman believes that contempt can single-handedly destroy relationships. Once a team member or someone in a relationship experiences contempt for another on a regular basis, that relationship is in serious trouble, according to Dr. Gottman. Contempt occurs when the interaction in a relationship slips into a vicious verbal attack or an intense emotional devaluation of the other person. Contempt displays itself with sarcasm, mocking, or irreverent tone of voice, rolling of the eyes, hostile or mean-spirited humor, or, at its most basic level, vicious name calling. Contempt is the most evil of all of the four horsemen and has the most serious effect on the relationship.

Contempt falls into basically two categories: verbal words, and emotions felt towards the other person.

Contemptuous words have no place in any relationship that you value. Name calling such as "idiot," "stupid," "you make me sick," and "you're nothing but a loser," explicitly humiliate or wound the other person. These words are toxic and indefensible. They will surely destroy a relationship.

The emotion of contempt occurs when a constant lack of respect toward the other individual(s) in the relationship is present. When there is a constant emotional thought process that devalues the other person in the relationship, even when the other person is not present, the horseman of contempt is at hand. **I cannot emphasize enough the danger of the poison of contempt.** It will singularly destroy a relationship or a team like a poison. If you find yourself contemptuous toward another person in a personal relationship or a professional relationship, realize you are deep into the cycle of dysfunction in this relationship. I encourage you to develop action steps that include getting help in some manner for this relationship or team. Don't delay—take action now.

TIPS FOR CONFLICT RESOLUTION

Here are some tips that can help you to resolve professional or personal conflict:

1. *Understand the other person's personality.* Take the time to understand the person with whom you are engaging in conflict. This will give you a heads-up on how they process information and how they are going to respond to you behaviorally during confrontations and resolutions.

2. *Choose the appropriate environment to enter into conflict resolution*. It is important to enter into a conflict conversation in a place that is both free from interruptions and where each person feels safe enough to speak freely.

3. *Engage in active listening.* Every person, regardless of his or her personality, desires to be heard. Active listening is engaging your mind and body in the listening process. This means paying attention to your nonverbal responses while staying focused on what the other person is saying. While this may go against your emotional impulsivity, choose to overcome your emotions by engaging in active listening.

4. *Keep the conflict conversation on the issue*. Avoid focusing on the person with whom you are in conflict, but instead continue to redirect the conversation to the issue at hand if necessary. Offer respect to the person regardless of whether you agree with his or her stance or not. If the conversation becomes emotional, stay calm and redirect the conversation to the problem. Remember to not criticize the person; rather, complain about the action.

5. *Take personal responsibility*. If the conflict calls for you to take responsibility for an action—do so. Take responsibility for your own behavior. This will open the door for conflict resolution, and it disarms the other members of the team or other person in the relationship with whom you are having the conflict conversation.

6. *Set realistic expectations.* Conflict resolution may be very difficult. Setting unrealistic expectations for yourself or others may cause more conflict in the future. Work toward a resolution that everyone can buy into; however, do not overpromise and under deliver. Once the resolution plan

has been set, commit to implementing it regardless if it is not "the perfect plan" in your mind.

7. ***End the conflict conversation with affirmation.*** Even if the conflict is not resolved within that first meeting and you both "agree to disagree," show integrity and character by offering affirmation and respect for the parties involved in the conflict conversation. Thank them for their openness and honesty. Commit to them that you will continue to offer your honest feedback in an effort to make this relationship or team better.

CHAPTER SEVEN

THE DNA RELATIONSHIP CONTINUUM

"The value of a relationship is in direct proportion to the time that you invest in the relationship."

—Brian Tracy

As you are well aware by now, this book is all about relationships. While relationships can be quite complex, developing successful relationship skills is not as difficult as it may seem. Healthy relationships require an investment. They also require reciprocation, or an ability to give and take. **Simply put, if you want a good relationship then you must take responsibility to create a good relationship.** The good news is that the skills needed to create a good relationship can be learned.

A major problem in developing healthy relationships is that we have bought into a common myth. This myth states that "if we feel it, we must express it or say it. And if we don't feel it, then we cannot express it or say it." **Having a healthy relationship is a choice. It is not an emotion.** It is choosing to be kind, compassionate, and considerate to those with whom we are in a relationship, whether that relationship is professional or personal. In other words, *if you don't feel it—then fake it*. I am not advocating manipulation. I am advocating taking personal responsibility for your words and your behavior as they relate to your significant relationships. I realize that this is controversial, and some individuals may not be able to get past the concept of "faking it." However, if your motives are pure and your desire is to develop a healthy, authentic relationship, then you must be responsible for your words and emotions.

For example: Let's suppose that I oversleep and am late for work. I jump out of bed and stub my toe while getting in the shower (I fight the anger that instinctually rises). While trying to drink coffee in my car on the way to work, I spill it when driving over a pothole, which leaves a large stain on my newly-purchased shirt and tie. I then realize that there are blue lights behind me, and I am pulled over and given a citation for speeding. Obviously, when I enter the office I am not having a good day, and am probably not in a good mood either. However, if I've truly invested in my team, in those with whom I live with, lead, and love, I have no right to expose them to my horrible disposition. Instead I choose to control my emotions and my words. While I may share my experience with them, I choose not to make my team members victims of my anger about my horrible morning. What I feel like saying and doing and how I actually behave are quite different.

I have, therefore, chosen to "fake it." With that being said, the ultimate goal of any relationship is to develop trust between the individuals within that relationship. We must realize that trust is something that is developed, not something that is gained instantaneously.

THE RELATIONSHIP TRIANGLE

So the question is this: How do we obtain true trust in a relationship or team? Upon conducting a small amount of research, you will soon find that there are numerous models and multiple tips on how to build a successful team or how to have a successful relationship. Through years of investigating and implementing these academic models, and through years and years of practical, hands-on experience, I have developed what I believe is a practical and relevant example for building a cohesive team and/or a fluid, healthy relationship.

Pictured above you will see a pyramid much like the food pyramid, though for our purposes we're going to call this example "The Relationship Triangle." At the base of this pyramid is the word *RESPECT.* The bottom layer is the foundation for a pyramid or triangle, and I believe that respect is the foundation of any relationship of any kind.

Consider this question: Is a relationship something that is earned or something that is given? All of my life I have been taught that we must earn the respect of others. And likewise, others must work to earn my respect. While I am not disputing that age-old truth, I am asking you to look at your relationships from a different perspective. I believe that respect in relationships is something that is given—not earned. We have a responsibility at the very core of our beings to respect someone simply because that someone is a person like ourselves. This unconditional respect is offered to everyone at the beginning of the relationship. The other persons' observed and experienced behavior in that relationship will dictate whether or not I respect their actions, their life, and who they are from a behavioral or achievement standpoint. However, the starting point of any relationship must be, "I choose to respect you as a human being." That is fundamentally where the relationship must begin. Once that occurs, the second component of a successful relationship can take place.

Think about your triangle again. Above the word Respect put the word *CONNECTION*. Connection occurs as the relationship begins to become fluid. This is not something that is tangible. You can't see it; you can only experience it. Connection happens when those on a team or in a relationship can begin to predict the behaviors, emotions, and capabilities of the other person/people on the team, and respond to those predictions with their own behaviors, emotional responses, and capabilities. This is not mind reading—it's a connection.

Connection in a relationship experiences safety, security, and stability. This means being able to depend on one another. Connection is the belief that each team member will pull his or her own weight. On a team, connection looks like a centralized vision, mission, core values, and goals. For a relationship, connection looks like sharing common values, common visions, and common goals. Once connectivity happens, team members have established a mutual respect for one another, and two people with connection have begun to experience fluidity in accomplishing the goals that are set before them, and the next step of the relationship process occurs.

Think of our triangle again. This time above the word Connection, put the word *AUTHENTICITY*. Once a team or relationship is connected and their processes become more fluid, they will begin to feel the freedom to be authentic. At this level personality differences are acknowledged and appreciated. Each team member becomes aware of the importance of diversity from a personality standpoint. Members realize that they can now voice opinions, share ideas, and address concerns while experiencing respect and active listening.

In relationships, both parties recognize the differences within their psychological makeup. Each person has the others' permission to be who he or she is and to celebrate the different approaches each one takes towards life. Understand that this is a very powerful phase in a relationship or team building. Developing an understanding of different personality types and learning how to communicate and resolve conflict are essential components to the success of a relationship, and will go a long way towards allowing authenticity within a team or personal relationship.

Being given the freedom to operate out of one's own strength set means there will be differences of opinion. Each person on the team or in the relationship can now freely express himself or herself without fear of being disconnected or disrespected.

Let's review our triangle:

We began the relationship triangle on a foundation of Respect. Because that Respect is given, Connection occurs next as people begin to buy into a common direction. This affords the freedom of Authenticity, where individuals can express views from their own personalities. This will lead to the next stage in the relationship, so on top of the word Authenticity in your triangle, place the word CONFLICT. As we have discussed in a previous chapter, conflict must occur if a team or a relationship is going to be healthy and successful. The ability to navigate healthy conflict is not a negative thing; it is a positive component of any team or relationship. Conflict must occur; it is where creativity is spawned, innovation is born, and real progress is made. Team leaders who only allow for "yes men" to participate tend to be weak minded and weak in their skill sets. A relationship that allows only one opinion to be expressed or implemented is not a relationship, but a dictatorship. Learn to embrace conflict and learn to experience conflict in a positive and healthy way.

Finally, at the very top of our triangle we find the word TRUST. It is my experience that trust must be earned. Trust does not equal instant gratification. It cannot be instantaneously given or received. Reaching the level of trust in a relationship or on a team takes work, intentionality, and time. Teams that have achieved this level of trust are teams that are highly successful, highly motivated, and can produce powerful outcomes together.

Relationships that have achieved the level of trust are those relationships that have stood the test of time and should be treasured as rare and precious jewels.

A FLOCK OF GEESE

I have learned in life that God provides many examples and learning opportunities for us if we simply take the time to observe what he has created. Let's take a moment to consider what we can learn from a flock of geese: Notice that geese fly in a V formation; each bird **respects** the wing span of the other. As an individual bird flaps its wings it creates an uplift for the bird following within the formation. **Respecting** the space of each individual bird allows the whole flock to add 71 percent greater flying range than if one bird flew alone. The geese fly in a V formation that is seamless, with each bird fully aware of its responsibility in this process. Whenever a goose falls out of formation it suddenly feels drag and resistance. Not only that, a quick observation reveals that the V is no longer fluid or **connected**. Once the bird gets back in the formation and is **connected** with the other birds, the lifting power of the entire V formation immediately increases.

The leadership position of the V is shared by each goose in the formation. When the lead goose gets tired it rotates to the back of the formation and another goose flies in at the point position. Therefore, each goose gets to share its **authentic** leadership skills with the entire flock. Not only that, but as the lead position rotates, so does each position within the formation. That means that each goose will experience and contribute its **authentic** gift set of flying from each position on the V formation.

While flying in formation, the geese consistently honk at one another. This honking is used to encourage and to sound the alarm of a dangerous situation. If the geese were silent and did not honk at one another, the chances of completing their flight journey would dramatically drop. Each bird has its own unique honk and sounds it in **conflict** with the other birds in flight. This sharing of

conflict combines to ensure a safe journey for the geese. Should a goose get sick, wounded, or shot down on their journey, two geese will drop out of the formation and follow it down to help protect it. They will stay with it until it is able to fly again, or dies. At that point they will launch out on their own creating another formation, or they will catch up with their original flock. This is a wonderful example of the commitment and **trust** each bird has with the others—choosing to fly together as well as protect one another through difficult times.

The result of establishing this powerful team is that geese can fly up to thirty thousand feet in the air. They can cross the Himalayan Mountains and can travel over five thousand miles in migration. Powerful relationships and powerful teams produce powerful results. Let's step back and use what we have already learned so far and see how it applies to the DNA Continuum.

DNA CONTINUUM

I have found that many times it is helpful to have a visual construct to practically apply relationship principles to our lives. In order to clearly express the DNA Continuum to you, I have chosen to use a very common four-quadrant continuum. I realize that there are multiple four-quadrant models out there; however, mine is designed to provide a simple and effective construct for improving relationships, on both an individual and a corporate scale.

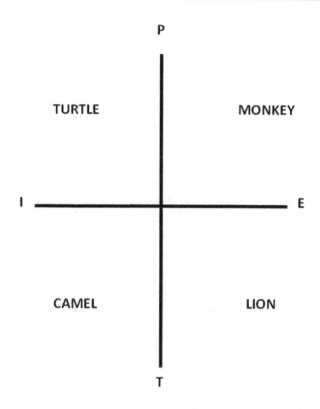

Let's take a look at two continuums, one horizontal and one vertical (think about an *x* and *y* axis on a graph). At the top (or north) of the vertical continuum is the letter "**P**" for PEOPLE. At the bottom, or south, of the vertical continuum is the letter "**T**" for TASK. On the horizontal continuum, the east side of the continuum is the letter "**E**" for EXTROVERT. On the far west side of the continuum there is an "**I**" for INTROVERT. I realize that we cannot label people with personality types that are accurate a hundred percent of the time. However, we can identify general tendencies that we have based on our personality makeup. Therefore, this continuum represents generalized definitions of the personality makeup of a relationship or of a team. In other words, each of us is uniquely different and thus has a unique position on the continuum. This position may change as we experience different life circumstances. Let me explain.

The top half of the horizontal continuum represents personalities who are people driven. The bottom half of the horizontal continuum represents personalities who are task driven. The "E" on the horizontal continuum represents personalities who are extroverted. An extrovert is defined as an "outgoing person or someone who is visibly self-confident." The "I," or Introverted, component of the continuum represents people who are defined as "reserved and who do not socialize to a great degree."

In general terms, looking at the top, right quadrant, someone who is people oriented and extroverted can be classified as a Much-Loved Monkey.

In the bottom, right quadrant belong people who are task driven and extroverted, otherwise known as Leading Lions.

People in the bottom, left quadrant are those who are task driven and introverted, and can be called Competent Camels.

In the top, left quadrant we find people who are person oriented and introverted, such as Tranquil Turtles.

The first step in effectively using the DNA Continuum is to identify your primary and secondary personality traits and place them on the continuum graph. Remember, even though two people may score as Much-Loved Monkeys, the continuum allows for each person to recognize his or her own unique personality. For example, some Monkeys may be more people oriented and less extroverted. Some Monkeys may have an inclination to be more outgoing and more task-driven.

For right now, let's focus on placing those we are graphing in the appropriate quadrants. It is important to place secondary personality traits in their corresponding quadrants, as well. For example, let's say that my high score was in the Much-Loved Monkey category, and my next highest score was in Tranquil Turtle. Looking at our DNA Continuum, I could ascertain that my personality makeup lies totally on the north side of the Horizontal Continuum. That means that while I may have a high level of people skills, I must choose to develop my task-oriented skill set.

I challenge you to take the time to graph the personality makeup of those with whom you are in a personal relationship, and I encourage you to also graph those with whom you have a professional relationship.

The tendency for most people is to stay within the comfort zone of their own quadrant. In other words, a person with a Lion personality may tend to communicate, navigate conflict, and define relationships all from the Lion quadrant. When this occurs the Lion is only effective when dealing with other Lions who understand the language that he is speaking. If we are going to make a difference in the lives of those we live with, love, or lead, we must choose to get out of the comfort zone of our own quadrant and enter into the quadrants of others.

For instance, if the Lion is going to develop an effective relationship with the Monkeys in her life, she must learn to speak the Monkeys' language. That means learning to laugh and connect with the Monkey as a person before focusing on the task. If she is to connect with Camels, that means she must choose to pay attention to the details in the relationship, and allow for structure and organization in the relationship process. If she is going to connect with Turtles, she must slow down and take the time to invest in things that are important to the Turtle.

WARNING

Getting out of your quadrant to invest in another's quadrant takes an incredible amount of emotional energy. I am often asked the question, "Which quadrant is most difficult for each personality to connect with?" While all quadrants take energy, generally the most difficult quadrant for a Lion to interact with is the Turtle quadrant, and vice versa. The most difficult quadrant for a Monkey to interact with is the Camel quadrant, and vice versa. The secret to successful relationships is not that we stay in our own quadrant, but that we learn to invest in other quadrants, accepting that this will cause us to drain our emotional energy.

Therefore, it is also good for us to spend time in our own quadrant to renew our souls. We must know what it means to renew our own emotional energy.

There is a difference between choosing to invest in other quadrants and expending emotional energy to try and become something we are not. Monkeys can never become Camels. However, Monkeys can invest in Camel-like behavior in order to connect with Camels. This will deplete Monkeys of their emotional and mental energy; therefore, Monkeys must also spend some time in their own quadrant renewing that energy.

So the question becomes, "How do we renew our emotional energy?" Monkeys renew their emotional energy with socialization, laughter, and fun. Lions renew their emotional energy through accomplishing tasks. Camels' emotional energy is renewed through operating within a controlled, organized, and structured environment. Turtles are renewed when they have time to think, observe, and relax. I think of the DNA relationship process as a dance. First you understand which quadrant you are most comfortable in, then you choose to get out of that quadrant and invest in the lives of those around you, then you jump back into your quadrant to renew your soul, but only so that you can leave your quadrant again in order to invest in other people, remembering to go back into your quadrant to renew your soul, so that you can leave your quadrant again in order to invest in other people . . . you get the idea. There is one fact that is certain: unless you choose to be intentional about investing in the lives of others, then you will not make a difference in their lives.

CHAPTER EIGHT

THE ESSENTIAL GIFT

"We are not put on earth for ourselves, but are placed here for each other."

—Jeff Warner

As you travel the journey of developing and growing both professional and personal relationships, there are some things that you must be made aware of if you are going to truly experience healthy relationships. More importantly, these essential gifts will allow you to make a difference in the lives of those you love, live with, and lead.

MONKEY ESSENTIALS

The following are essential guidelines if you are in a personal or professional relationship with a Monkey. The quickest way to destroy a relationship with a Monkey is to give consistent negative feedback to him or her. Monkeys have exceptional people skills and will not tolerate someone who makes them feel guilty, ashamed, or devalued. Because of their sensitivity and tendency to be impulsive, Monkeys will quickly distance themselves from negative or critical people. Then they will avoid contact with these people on a personal or professional level. If the Monkey cannot avoid contact, he will build an emotional wall and become guarded and irritable.

Once a Monkey is hurt emotionally, she can forgive the offender if that person offers a sincere, heartfelt apology. However, if the person continues to emotionally hurt the Monkey, then she will disassociate herself emotionally and physically from the offender.

"I can't believe he left after twenty-five years of marriage!" Stephanie was in tears during one of their marital counseling sessions. "We have a nice home; we have two children and three grandchildren. How could he just up and leave? Everything was going as planned. We had our retirement portfolio in order, our house mortgage nearly paid off; our debt was almost zero . . . and then he just up and leaves! It makes no sense!"

Stephanie the Camel was married to Jason the Monkey, and for twenty-five years she had been in a relationship that was difficult at times and functional at others. They were believers who were active in their church and community. Stephanie literally never saw the divorce coming. She assumed that because all of the tasks of the marriage were taken care of, everything was just fine. That was a bad assumption. While Stephanie found her security in the planned and organized details of the family responsibilities, Jason was slowly building walls and blocking her out of his life emotionally. He learned early in the relationship to stop being vulnerable. Showing any kind of weakness or lack of planned process brought criticism from his spouse. Therefore, he turned his attention to his job, his children, and his hobbies of playing cards, drinking a beer with his buddies, and his golf game. His emotional needs remained unmet, and he joined the thousands of married couples who live their lives in the rut of day-to-day routine. Jason discovered that in providing well for the family financially and taking care of the maintenance needs of the home he could keep Stephanie's criticism to a somewhat-tolerable level.

Stephanie realized that there was an emotional disconnect between Jason and herself, but she chalked it up to Jason's just being "a man." She found support from her female friends and stayed extremely busy, caring for the children, her job, and keeping the household organized and running smoothly.

Stephanie had no idea that her husband had emotional needs that were unmet. In her mind, they had made a commitment to each other, and there was no option but to keep their promise to stay married. She was committed to following the rules regardless of the cost.

Jason, on the other hand, had followed the rules for twenty-five years, and while he knew that the rules say that divorce is wrong, he simply could not live the last season of his life with a woman he no longer loved. Their relationship had become emotionally void and in his mind had fallen into a relationship of obligation. Jason needed more and was not going to stay in a relationship that was shrouded in negativity and criticism. He was determined to find someone to love who could accept him as he was.

Fortunately, this couple chose to get the help they desperately needed. Thus they began the process of understanding how to love and lead one another. Stephanie the Camel learned how to love Jason the Monkey and Jason learned how to give Stephanie the love she needed as well. They became aware of their own personality tendencies and then learned about each other's personalities. Each made a conscious decision to get out of his or her own personality quadrant and offer the essential gifts of validation to the other. With both Stephanie and Jason investing in one another, their relationship began to heal. While they still struggle from time to time (as all relationships do), Jason and Stephanie are now struggling together instead of separately, and are continuing to make a difference in each other's life.

When you enter a professional or personal relationship with a Monkey, remember their approach to life: They desire variety and excitement, and they embrace change. Monkeys love positive surprises and new experiences. They love to try things that have not been tried before, and cherish the concept of brainstorming creative solutions to obstacles.

Monkeys will flourish with verbal feedback and positive reinforcement. If their environment turns into a routine, they will find it boring; if their environment is fast-paced and fun, they will love it! So mix it up for your Monkey, introduce new things, and tell him or her how much they are appreciated.

If you love, live with, or lead a Monkey, here are the essential gifts that will allow you to make a difference in his or her life:

- Keep eye contact with the Monkey. This shows that you are engaged in the conversation and care about him or her.

- Remember that Monkeys are extroverts. They love to brainstorm and problem-solve verbally. This means that the conversation may drift from its original intent as the Monkey gets new ideas or becomes unfocused on the issue at hand.

- Monkeys take criticism very personally. Be sure when you disagree or disapprove that you communicate clearly that you still value the Monkey. Clarify that you are disapproving of the issue, not the person.

- Monkeys receive validation from words. They also receive rejection from words or the lack of words. Words are powerful tools that can encourage or discourage Monkeys.

- Conversations with Monkeys will often turn playful, as Monkeys enjoy sharing humor and use it as a way of connecting with one another. Appreciate the humor, and you appreciate the Monkey.

- Monkeys need appropriate touch. This may come in the form of a handshake, hug, or even a pat on the back. Touch indicates that "I like you and I approve of you." It is important to remember to be sensitive to those who are not comfortable with touch.

- Focus on personal interactions with Monkeys. Be aware of your verbal and nonverbal communication signals. It's not just what you communicate, but how you communicate that is important to Monkeys.

- Finally, know that Monkeys are validated, encouraged, and motivated by the approval and affirmation of others.

LION ESSENTIALS

The following are essential guidelines if you are in a personal or professional relationship with a Lion. The quickest way to destroy a relationship with a Lion is to attack his or her ego. Lions tend to have the largest egos and want to believe they are capable of accomplishing incredible tasks. Once a Lion's ego is destroyed, it is very difficult for that Lion to continue in the relationship with the destroyer. Lions will not pursue or invest in a relationship that devalues their ability to succeed. Therefore, the worst thing someone can do to a Lion is to disparage his ego or his ability to accomplish or conquer. Once the Lion's ego has been broken, the likelihood of the relationship's continuing in a healthy manner is slim. The Lion will generally turn to other areas or relationships that validate his ego and his ability to achieve.

"He is such a jerk. Did you see how he just treated Amber?" Jack asked angrily. Matt agreed. "We have to do something. I don't care that he has the highest sales numbers on the team; the way he treats all of us is inexcusable. We are just as important as he is."

Lloyd the Lion had produced incredible sales numbers after joining the Markets Incorporated sales team. He was aggressive, arrogant, and extremely focused on the task of making money. In fact, he was totally driven by money.

While the company had established a vision statement and mission statement, they both meant little to Lloyd. After all, they had hired him to make money; that was the bottom line. He read through the touchy-feely vision and mission statements of the company which had something to do with "making a difference in the lives of others," and he dutifully endured company meetings where the leadership team reminded its employees that the company operated around the core values of integrity and trust. Lloyd rolled his eyes when the CEO reminded the employees that they were all a family in this small company. Lloyd knew why he was there: because he could out-produce anybody, anytime, anywhere. His "mission" statement was *Show me the money.*

Lloyd's presence on the team had caused much chaos. At first the leadership team thought that his aggressive nature might serve as motivation to the other employees, but it soon became evident that Lloyd's behavior was having the opposite effect: the other employees disdained Lloyd's lack of concern for anyone but himself. For the others, coming to work became a difficult chore, as the thought of being around his arrogance was incredibly discouraging. This resulted in the rest of the sales team looking for reasons not to come to work. What they had loved about their company was now gone. Instead of working as a team that navigated times that were good and bad together, their culture had changed them into a team made up of silos with a cut-throat mentality. The matrix and benchmarks that had been established to promote ownership and accountability were no longer effective. Lloyd's poison of "every man for himself" was spreading throughout the team.

The result was that while Lloyd's numbers were up, the rest of the team's numbers were stagnant or even down. Besides that, Markets Incorporated was at risk of becoming hypocritical claiming that they were about making a difference in the lives of others while allowing love of the dollar to drive their decision-making process. It was at this point that the CEO had a serious decision to make. He could destroy Lloyd's ego and fire him, or he could attempt to lead Lloyd to change his approach. The CEO chose the latter.

The CEO had a hard conversation with Lloyd that went like this: "Lloyd, I know that you're a great salesman. Your numbers are incredible, and you have the ability to accomplish much in the area of sales with our company. However, Markets Incorporated has made a commitment to make a difference in the lives of others, and that starts with our employee family. I want you to know that we have committed to honoring this vision, even if it means sacrificing short-term financial gain. I know that you can operate within our culture, but you must choose to refrain from the way you look at yourself and others."

Because of this honest, direct approach, Lloyd the Lion made the right decision. He invested in a learning process that included personality awareness and gaining essential tools for making a difference in the lives of others. While Lloyd is still a Lion, he has chosen to buy into the concept of creating a long-term culture that will yield long-term results as well as healthy relationships. The rest of the sales team was encouraged by Lloyd's efforts, and now has a greater respect and tolerance for his strong ego.

As you grow or develop a personal or professional relationship with Lions, remember their approach to life: they are fast-paced, bottom line, "make it happen" people. Lions are direct, assertive, demanding, and strong-willed. They are driven, and tend to be impulsive, with strong personalities and strong egos.

Lions can quickly become angry; however, they also tend to get over things quickly. Lions think of life as a series of events with each event standing on its own, separate from other events. They do not want to be weighted down with too many details or excessive talk when a decision needs to be made. Lions just want to pull the trigger. Lions are very competitive and have no problem taking charge of a situation. Lions focus more on results than the process.

If you love, live with, or lead a Lion, here are the essential gifts that will allow you to make a difference in his or her life:

- When speaking to a Lion, be strong and confident with your language. Remember that Lions respect strength.

- Lions do not respect an overload of details. Frame your thought processes for "big picture" thinking and communicating.

- Communicate to the Lion that you acknowledge and appreciate his or her ability to achieve. The Lion does not care if you like him, but *is* concerned with the respect you show toward his position and ability to achieve the given task.

- Lions think in a win/lose frame of mind. Be careful not to engage the Lion's competitive nature. Lions do not respond well to threats or challenges.

- Lions may come across as rude. Remember, Lions do not *think* of themselves as rude, but rather as someone who speaks what they perceive to be the truth.

- Do not take the words of a Lion personally. Lions are task-driven, and use words only as tools for accomplishing the task.

- Know that Lions are validated, encouraged, and motivated by respect, empowerment, and the accomplishment of the task.

Camel Essentials

The following are essential guidelines if you are in a personal or professional relationship with a Camel. The quickest way to destroy a relationship with a Camel is to withdraw all structure and organization from the relationship. Camels are analytical, detail-driven, and process-oriented. They will not tolerate someone who does not consistently play by the rules or who is totally unpredictable and displays no dependability. Because of their need to process all the facts and develop a thorough plan before proceeding, Camels will feel invalidated and become extremely frustrated with those who "fly by the seat of their pants" on a consistent basis. An unstructured environment causes a Camel to feel out of control. When a Camel feels out of control, he or she will become extremely critical and remove himself or herself from the environment if at all possible. Camels have a problem understanding emotional people. However, they are willing to help from a task perspective in any given crisis. Because Camels are introverted, they may have a difficult time articulating the right words to someone who is going through an emotionally difficult time.

"I thought we had agreed to meet at 2:00 p.m.," Kimberly explained. "As usual, you refuse to keep your word."

"What? It's only 2:15," said Lindsey "How can you be so anal? I stopped to pick up a paper at the news stand and had the nicest chat with the sales lady. I just love walking through the city; so many people and so many new things to see every day!"

"Lindsey, can we just get busy planning the family reunion? You know the importance of this one. I have another meeting in ninety-seven minutes and I have to travel six blocks to get there," said Kimberly.

The two sisters had always been different. Kimberly was a serious-minded planner, and Lindsey was a happy-go-lucky, free spirit. Now that they were adults they rarely spent time together because they both got on each other's last nerve. In fact, they wouldn't be together now except for this "one last family reunion," as they now knew it: their father was dying with a diagnosis of a terminal disease. The doctors had given him less than a year to live. He had requested that the family get together one more time. The task had fallen to Kimberly and Lindsey to plan, organize, and implement the family reunion.

Kimberly had arrived at the designated coffee shop thoroughly prepared. She had her notebook, her calendar, her contact list of all family members, and a list of possible locations for the event. Lindsey, on the other hand, showed up empty-handed, late, and seemingly unconcerned about this monumental occasion that they were planning.

The meeting degenerated quickly. Kimberly asked, "Lindsey, did you bring your contact list of family members that I asked you to bring?"

Lindsey responded, "I have them in my head."

Kimberly rolled her eyes and asked, "Did you bring a notebook, pen, or calendar?" As she spoke Kimberly realized that Lindsey had nothing in her hand except for the newspaper she had just purchased at the newsstand. "Lindsey, you came totally unprepared! If you are going to plan a successful family reunion then you must have an organized plan and process! Otherwise, something will not get covered, and this will not be how we want our last family reunion with our dad to be remembered. I have worked diligently to gather contact information, location information, and pricing on catering. And you, what exactly have you done, Lindsey?"

"Well, it looks like you have everything covered," Lindsey responded. "Obviously you don't need my input or anyone else's. You have it planned and organized already. Tell you what, why don't you do this family reunion thing by yourself? I'm sure anything I could contribute would not meet your expectations anyway."

And with that, Lindsey stood up and left her still-full cup of coffee and Kimberly sitting at the table as she stomped out of the coffee shop.

Later that evening her mother asked Lindsey how the meeting went that afternoon.

"About as horrible as a meeting could go," Lindsey said. "I know I could have been better prepared, but Kimberly's rigid nature and inflexible attitude make it almost impossible to work with her."

Their mother smiled and said, "I realize how different the two of you are. In fact, I was so concerned about it that I began to investigate the concept of personality awareness. I want you to take some time to educate yourself on the diversity of personality makeup. I want you to become aware of your temperament and tendencies as well as those of other people. You see, the issue is not that you and Kimberly don't love each other. The issue is you simply can't speak one another's language. The good news is each personality language can be learned.

Lindsey took her mother at her word and spent the next several days researching and reading about personality diversity. This educational process allowed Lindsey to realize that no one personality was right and no one personality was wrong. It allowed her to build a tolerance for her sister's personality and gave her the tools to connect with her sister in an effective way. Consequently Lindsey called Kimberly to offer her sincere apology for frustrating her sister and asked that they schedule another meeting. She explained to Kimberly that she had researched why they had had such a difficult time connecting with each other through the years. She offered to share her insight with her sister at their next meeting.

Lindsey arrived fifteen minutes early for their meeting and had prepared an outline of the research she had conducted. She also brought with her a calendar and a written contact list of family members. This awareness turned the corner in the relationship of the two sisters. They worked together to plan the last family reunion for their dad that honored his legacy. They also began a new journey of creating their own legacy of sisters who loved each other and who made a difference in one another's life.

When you enter a professional or personal relationship with a Camel, remember their approach to life: they are slower paced, and they focus on the process rather than the results. Camels love predictability, and they are not fond of spontaneity. Camels will flourish when given all of the details of a given situation. If the environment is one that offers stability and structure then Camels will love it. Camels are careful, cautious, and organized people. Give your Camel a plan. Allow him or her to follow that plan to completion, and you will have one happy Camel.

If you love, live with, or lead a Camel, here are the essential gifts that will allow you to make a difference in his or her life:

- Use the Boy Scout motto and "always be prepared" when communicating with a Camel.

- Be ready to answer multiple questions about multiple details.

- Outlines and organized documentation allow the Camel to feel in control and self-assured.

- Talk in rational terms to Camels. Remember, a Camel does not respond to emotional conversations.

- When presenting a Camel with a new idea or concept, give him or her time to process the information.

- Never ask the Camel to break the rules. Violating rules is against the very nature of their being. Remember that Camels set unrealistic expectations for themselves and for all those around them. Therefore, help your Camel to set appropriate expectations for themselves and others that are reasonable and can be met.

- Finally, know that Camels are validated, encouraged, and motivated through organized, detailed processes with an emphasis on the quality of the task.

TURTLES ESSENTIALS

The following are the essential guidelines if you are in a personal or professional relationship with a Turtle. The quickest way to destroy a relationship with a Turtle is to create an environment of conflict, chaos, and strife. Turtles are laid back, warm, and friendly, and will not tolerate someone who makes them feel constantly rushed or belittled, or who threatens those with whom the Turtle has established a deep relationship. Because of their nice and polite manner, some would perceive the Turtle as being weak, or a "doormat." This would be a critical mistake. Turtles will attack with full force, and of all of the four personalities are the ones most likely to hurt you should you attempt to hurt a relationship that they love. Turtles also tend to have the most difficulty overcoming hurts that have been done to them. Once they feel that they have been hurt or that someone has been disloyal, their memories are long, and reconciliation is very difficult, and sometimes even a rare occurrence. Trust for the Turtle is not easily given, and is even more difficult to rebuild.

"I just don't understand it. How could the meeting have gone that bad? I addressed all the different options we could take," said Joseph, the Vice President of Operations of a large, international corporation. Joseph was describing to his executive coach a meeting he had with his CEO to flesh out a significant strategy that was to be led and implemented by Joseph's team for the entire company.

"It was as if he couldn't hear what I was saying," Joseph said. "He seemed agitated and frustrated. He cut me off several times to ask me to get to the point, but the entire presentation *was* the point!"

Joseph was referring to Mr. Barnes, the CEO of the company, who happened to be a thoroughbred Lion. Joseph continued. "At one point I noticed that he wasn't even listening. He was reading emails on his blackberry. I left that meeting feeling demoralized, discouraged, and doubting my position as a vice president of this company."

"Let's take a look at your presentation," said his executive coach. Joseph had taken several weeks to think carefully about the different options available for the project. He had pulled his team together a few days before the deadline to help create the presentation, most of whom were Camels, and they had developed several very lengthy and detailed strategies to present to their CEO. As the executive coach reviewed the presentation he realized that, sadly, Joseph had set himself up for defeat before he ever entered the CEO's office.

Joseph's executive coach said, "Joseph, I want us to put the presentation on hold for now, and I want to ask you to conduct a study on personality awareness. I want you to become aware of your personality tendencies and see if you can determine what it was that your boss was looking for from your presentation. See if you can identify areas that might trigger a positive response from Mr. Barnes." Because of the relationship and trust developed between the executive coach and Joseph, he agreed with this plan.

Joseph soon discovered powerful tools not only for help in communicating with his boss, Mr. Barnes, but for help in communicating and understanding the relationships in his life. Through his educational process, Joseph discovered that his boss was straightforward and results driven, not detail driven. His leadership style was to entrust those around him to cover the details so that he could set the course and direction for the company. Mr. Barnes was not as interested in how the strategy was to be implemented or the different strategy options that existed as he was in knowing that there was a general plan in place. Joseph realized his error; he had shown his boss many potential options and complicated strategies for executing each one. He had not shown Mr. Barnes what he wanted to see: a clear, direct picture of what was going to happen in the long term.

Joseph learned how to speak "Lion talk" when presenting to Mr. Barnes. He threw phrases such as "maybe," "I should," "perhaps we might," "I think," "we might," or "it appears that" out of his vocabulary. He replaced them with strong phrases such as "I will," "we can," "we are going to," etc. Joseph called his team around him once again and walked the team through his personality awareness insight. Then he led them to reconstruct the entire strategy roll-out presentation for Mr. Barnes. Joseph scheduled another meeting with Mr. Barnes with a promise to be in and out of his office within thirty minutes. The next meeting was short, precise, and efficient, with many fewer slides and way fewer bullet points and details attached. Mr. Barnes was impressed. Consequently, Joseph's status has risen as a leader that Mr. Barnes can count on to get results. More importantly, Joseph has learned the secret of relating to and thus making a difference in the lives of those he lives with, leads, and loves.

When you enter into a professional or personal relationship with Turtles, remember their approach to life. They are caring people who are deeply committed to family, tradition, and loyalty. Turtles are deliberate, yet can prove to be very flexible when the situation calls for flexibility. They desire deep relationships and flourish in an unhurried environment. While Turtles are introverts, they present a welcoming, easy-to-approach temperament. Turtles are a great example of the saying, "Still waters run deep." Don't assume because your Turtle looks like she is on an even kilt that there is little going on inside of her emotionally. So, connect with your Turtle. Take the time to build that deep relationship which will equal validation for your Turtle.

If you love, live with, or lead a Turtle, here are the essential gifts that will allow you to make a difference in his or her life:

- Remember to be patient. Turtles move at their own pace in their own time.

- Turtles do not respond to chaos, but instead to calm and peace.

- Turtles are not verbal; therefore, a nod or a non-comment from a Turtle does not necessarily mean that she agrees with you.

- Use your ears. Turtles are great listeners, but taking the time to listen to the Turtle can result in incredible wisdom being given to you.

- Do not be impulsive when communicating with a Turtle.

- Remember that Turtles respond to safe, low-risk environments.

- Guide a Turtle to overcome his or her tendency to procrastinate by giving timelines with accountability built in.

- Finally, know that Turtles are validated, encouraged, and motivated when you focus on what is truly important to the Turtle—significant relationships that they have established with those they love or are loyal to, in other words, the one-on-one interpersonal relationships.

CHAPTER NINE

CONCLUDING THOUGHTS

"Go out into the world today and love the people you meet.
Let your presence light new light in the hearts of people."
—Mother Teresa

A little boy was walking down the street when he decided to enter the local pet store. He soon found himself in the very back of the store looking down into a small bin that held the store's puppies. His eyes were drawn to one particular puppy that he knew he had to have. Immediately he went to the store owner and asked the price of the puppy. Once he knew the price of the puppy, the little boy immediately left the pet store determined to raise the money needed to purchase his puppy. For the next week the little boy did anything he could do to earn money. He swept the sidewalk, washed the car, and found various other odd jobs in which he could earn a small wage.

Once the little boy had secured the amount needed for his purchase, he hurried back to the pet store, went straight to the back, and found the puppy that he had worked so hard to have. He took the puppy in his arms and walked to the front counter of the pet store. He placed his money on the counter and headed for the door. When the owner noticed the particular puppy that the boy had chosen, he stopped the boy as he was leaving.

"Son, wait just a minute," the owner said. "You don't want that puppy. That puppy has a crippled leg. A young, strong boy like you needs a puppy that is able to run and play with you. That puppy you

have right there is damaged goods. Let me have it back and we can swap it for another puppy."

"No sir," the little boy replied, "this is the exact puppy I want!"

The owner began to protest, but stopped suddenly as his eyes were drawn to the brace on the little boy's leg. The little boy knew full well that this puppy would never be able to run or jump. He understood exactly how the little fellow felt. Just as the little boy struggled through life, he would help his puppy struggle as well. That little boy made a conscious decision to make a difference in the life of another.

That is one of my favorite stories, and I wanted to share it with you as we draw this journey of Personality Awareness to a close. The truth is that all of us have braces on our legs—we all have areas of weakness that cause us to stumble or struggle. We all experience difficult times and find ourselves in difficult situations. The message of this book and the message that I want to leave with you is that no matter who you are, no matter where you are, no matter what you are, you can choose to invest in the lives of others. You can improve your relationships, and thus your own life.

I love the beach. I have visited numerous beaches in my lifetime, and each one is unique and different, yet powerful and inspirational. In fact, much of this book was penned while I was on a get-away trip with my wife at the beach. It is amazing to me how vastly different the beach presents itself in a very short amount of time. You can wake up in the morning to a loud thunderstorm with the waves crashing violently upon the shore then find yourself that very same afternoon watching a beautiful sunset on a clear blue sky as small waves trickle onto the sand. The same is true with our lives. We will experience many different people in many different environments, and if we are blessed, we will live to see many seasons change in our lives.

I understand that what has been presented in this book is not an instant gratification or a quick-fix answer to all of your relationship problems. However, you have in your hand a set of tools for you to use to create your own individual relationships in your own unique way. My personal mission is to make a difference in the lives of people. It is my desire and my prayer that this book facilitates and supports that mission.

Finally, I ask that should you find a nugget or two of helpful information in the pages of this work, please share it with others. I am excited about your new journey towards developing successful and healthy relationships.

You can make a difference in the lives of those you love, live with, and lead.

WORKS CITED

Block, J. (1971). *Lives through time*. Berkeley, CA: Bancroft books.

Block, J. *The Q-sort method in personality assessment and psychiatric research*. Palo Alto, Calif.: Consulting Psychologists, 1978. (Originally published 1961.)

Gottman, John (1995). *Why Marriages Succeed or Fail: And How You Can Make Yours Last*. Simon & Schuster

Jung, C. G. (1976). *Psychological types*. Princeton, NJ: Princeton University Press

Keirsey, D. (1998). Please Understand Me II. Delmar, California: Prometheus Nemesis Books.

Myers, I. B., McCauUey, M. H., Quenk, N. L., & Hammer, A. L. (1998). *MBTI manual: A guide to the development and use of the Myers-Briggs Type Indicator* (3rd ed.). Palo Alto, CA: Consulting Psychologists Press.

Quotes retrieved from *Thinkexist.com Quotations* (1999-2011).

Made in the USA
Las Vegas, NV
31 January 2022

42742694R00062